Cambodian–Vietnamese War

Cambodian–Vietnamese War

Chapter 1 : Short History

The Cambodian–Vietnamese War referred to in Vietnam as the Counter-offensive on the Southwestern fringe, was an outfitted clash between the Socialist Republic of Vietnam and Democratic Kampuchea. The war started with secluded conflicts along the land and oceanic limits of Vietnam and Kampuchea somewhere in the range of 1975 and 1978, once in a while including division-sized military arrangements. On 25 December 1978, Vietnam propelled a full-scale intrusion of Kampuchea and in this manner involved the nation and expelled the legislature of the Communist Party of Kampuchea from control.

During the Vietnam War, Vietnamese and Cambodian socialists had shaped a partnership to battle U.S.- upheld systems in their individual nations. In spite of their open showcase of participation with the Vietnamese, the Khmer Rouge authority expected that the Vietnamese socialists were conspiring to shape an Indochinese league with Vietnam as the prevailing power in the district. So as to seize an endeavor by the Vietnamese to rule them, the Khmer Rouge administration started cleansing Vietnamese-prepared faculty inside their own positions as the Lon Nol system abdicated in 1975. At that point, in May 1975, the recently shaped Democratic Kampuchea, ruled by the Khmer Rouge, started assaulting Vietnam, starting with an assault on the Vietnamese island of Phú Quốc.

Regardless of the battling, the pioneers of reunified Vietnam and Kampuchea made a few open political trades all through 1976 to feature the evidently solid relations between them. Be that as it may, in the background, Kampuchean pioneers kept on dreading what they saw as Vietnamese expansionism. Thusly, on 30 April 1977, they propelled another significant military assault on Vietnam. Stunned by the Kampuchean ambush, Vietnam propelled a retaliatory strike toward the finish of 1977 trying to compel the Kampuchean government to arrange. In January 1978 the Vietnamese military pulled back on the grounds that their political targets had not been accomplished; the Khmer Rouge stayed reluctant to haggle genuinely.

Little scale battling proceeded between the two nations all through 1978, as China attempted to intervene harmony talks between the different sides. Nonetheless, neither one of the countries would consent to an adequate trade off. Before the finish of 1978, Vietnamese pioneers chose to evacuate the Khmer Rouge-commanded system of Democratic Kampuchea, seeing it as being ace Chinese and antagonistic towards Vietnam. On 25 December 1978, 150,000 Vietnamese soldiers attacked Democratic Kampuchea and overran the Kampuchean Revolutionary Army in only two weeks, along these lines finishing the overabundances of Pol Pot's system, which had been liable for the passings of very nearly a fourth of all Cambodians among 1975 and December 1978. Vietnamese military mediation and the possessing powers' consequent permitting in of worldwide nourishment help to moderate the enormous starvation is seen as completion the Cambodian genocide.

On 8 January 1979 the master Vietnamese People's Republic of Kampuchea (PRK) was built up in Phnom Penh, denoting the start of a ten-year Vietnamese occupation. During that period, the Khmer Rouge's Democratic Kampuchea kept on being perceived by the United Nations as the real administration of Kampuchea, as a few equipped opposition bunches were framed to battle the Vietnamese occupation. Off camera, Prime Minister Hun Sen of the PRK system moved toward groups of the Coalition Government of Democratic Kampuchea (CGDK) to start harmony talks. Under strategic and financial tension from the global network, the Vietnamese government executed a progression of monetary and international strategy changes, which prompted their withdrawal from Kampuchea in September 1989.

At the Third Jakarta Informal Meeting in 1990, under the Australian-supported Cambodian Peace Plan, agents of the CGDK and the PRK consented to a power-sharing course of action by framing a solidarity government known as the Supreme National Council (SNC). The SNC's job was to speak to Cambodian sway on the worldwide stage, while the United Nations Transitional Authority in Cambodia (UNTAC) was entrusted with overseeing the nation's local strategies until a Cambodian government was chosen by the individuals. Cambodia's pathway to harmony demonstrated to be troublesome, as Khmer Rouge pioneers chose not to take part in the general races, yet rather they decided to disturb the discretionary procedure by propelling military assaults on UN peacekeepers and executing ethnic Vietnamese vagrants. In any case, the CPP authority wouldn't acknowledge thrashing, and they declared that the eastern areas of Cambodia, where the greater part of the CPP's votes were drawn from, would withdraw from Cambodia. To keep away from such a result, Norodom Ranariddh, the pioneer of FUNCINPEC, consented to shape an alliance government with the CPP. In no time afterwards, the sacred government was reestablished and the Khmer Rouge was banned by the recently framed Cambodian government.

Angkor, the seat of the Khmer Empire, was exposed to Vietnamese impact as ahead of schedule as the thirteenth century. Vietnamese impact spread bit by bit and in a roundabout way, and it was not until the mid nineteenth century that Vietnam practiced direct control.

However, Vietnam's endeavors to transform Cambodia into their territory started in seventeenth century when Vietnamese powers helped Cambodian dissenters topple its solitary Muslim King, Ramathipadi I. From that point on, Vietnam as often as possible mediated in Cambodia. In 1813, Nak Ong Chan picked up the Cambodian honored position with the assistance of Vietnam, and under his standard Cambodia turned into a protectorate. Throughout the 1830s, Vietnam endeavored to eradicate Khmer culture, which had inferred the premise of Cambodian culture, dress, and religion from India as opposed to China. The pattern of Vietnamese predominance kept during French colonization, under which Cambodia had to surrender quite a bit of its southern area (which would later be Saigon, the Mekong Delta and Tây Ninh) to the Vietnamese. The Khmer Rouge later supported their invasions into Vietnam as an endeavor to recapture the domains which Cambodia had lost during the past centuries.

1.1 Rise of communism

The socialist development in Cambodia and Vietnam started before World War II with the establishing of the Indochinese Communist Party (ICP), solely commanded by the Vietnamese, initially intended to battle French pilgrim rule in Indochina. In 1941, Nguyen Ai Quoc (usually known by his nom de plume Ho Chi Minh) established the Viet Nam Doc Lap Dong Minh Hoi, or the Viet Minh. At the point when the Japanese were vanquished toward the finish of World War II, he started the first Indochinese war of freedom against the French. During this time, Vietnamese powers an utilized Cambodian area to move weapons, supplies, and troops. This relationship kept going all through the Vietnam War, when Vietnamese socialists utilized Cambodia as a vehicle course and arranging territory for assaults on South Vietnam. In 1951, Vietnam guided the foundation of a different Cambodian socialist gathering, the Kampuchean People's Revolutionary Party (KPRP), which aligned with a patriot dissenter Cambodian development, the Khmer Serei , so as to seek after freedom. As per the 1954 Geneva Accords arranging the finish of the French control, recently made socialist North Vietnam pulled the entirety of its Viet Minh troopers and units out of Cambodia; notwithstanding, since the KPRP was staffed principally by ethnic Vietnamese or Cambodians under its tutelage, around 5,000 socialist frameworks went with them.

The power vacuum the Vietnamese socialists left afterward in Cambodia was before long filled by the arrival of a youthful gathering of Cambodian socialist progressives, a significant number of whom got their socialist training in France. In 1960, the KPRP changed its name to the Kampuchean Communist Party (KCP), and the name was later embraced by the lion's share alliance that conformed to Saloth Sar (Pol Pot), Ieng Sary, and Khieu Samphan as the genuine political foundation memorializing the KCP . This club turned into the beginning of the Khmer Rouge, and its principle was intensely impacted by Maoist belief system.

1.2 Lon Nol's anti-Vietnamese sentiment

After the expulsion of Sihanouk from control in March 1970, the pioneer of the new Khmer Republic, Lon Nol, notwithstanding being enemy of socialist and apparently in the "professional American" camp, sponsored the FULRO against all Vietnamese, both enemy of socialist South Vietnam and the socialist Viet Cong. Lon Nol arranged a butcher of every single Vietnamese individuals in Cambodia and a restoration of South Vietnam to a resuscitated Champa state. Many were butchered and dumped in the Mekong River at the hands of Lon Nol's enemy of socialist forces. The Khmer Rouge later imitated Lon Nol's actions.

1.3 Democratic Kampuchea and the Khmer Rouge

The Khmer Rouge government embraced the secretive term Angkar, or 'the association', and the personalities of its pioneers stayed classified until 1977. The official head of state was Khieu Samphan, however the two men in charge of the gathering were Pol Pot and Ieng Sary. a definitive target of the Khmer Rouge was to delete the structure of the Cambodian state, which they saw as medieval, entrepreneur, and serving the motivation of both the landholding world class and colonialists. In its place, they planned to make an uncouth society dependent on laborer workers. The extreme belief systems and objectives of the Khmer Rouge were outsider ideas to the masses. The communist upset held almost no famous intrigue, which drove Pol Pot and his units to utilize ultra-patriot sentiment, severe and lethal standard, and propaganda planned for deriding the Vietnamese to keep up control.

Indeed, even before the Vietnam War finished, the connection between the Khmer Rouge—which was holding onto control from a US-supported system headed by Lon Nol—and North Vietnam was stressed. Conflicts between Vietnamese socialists and Khmer Rouge powers started as right on time as 1974, and the next year Pol Pot marked a bargain classifying the "companionship" between the Khmer Rouge and China.

Chapter 2 : Diplomacy and military action

The Fall of Phnom Penh and the Fall of Saigon in April 1975 quickly brought another contention among Vietnam and Cambodia. Despite the fact that the North Vietnamese and the Khmer Rouge had recently battled one next to the other, the pioneers of the recently made Democratic Kampuchea kept on review Vietnam with extraordinary doubt, since they accepted the Vietnamese socialists had never surrendered their fantasy about making an Indochinese organization with Vietnam as the leader. For that reason, the Kampuchean government evacuated all North Vietnamese military powers from Kampuchean territory not long after their catch of Phnom Penh on 17 April 1975. In the main significant conflict between the two previous partners, the Kampuchean Revolutionary Army (KRA) attacked the Vietnamese island of Phú Quốc on 1 May 1975, guaranteeing it was a piece of Kampuchea's territory.

After nine days, on 10 May 1975, the KRA proceeded with its attack by catching the Tho Chu Islands, where it executed 500 Vietnamese regular folks. In June 1975, while on a visit to Hanoi, Pol Pot recommended that

Vietnam and his nation should sign a settlement of companionship and start exchanges on fringe debates. In August 1975, Vietnam restored the island of Koh Wai to Kampuchea and officially perceived Kampuchean power over the island.

Following those occurrences, the two nations endeavored to improve their discretionary relations with a progression of congratulatory messages and trade visits. On 17 April 1976, Vietnamese pioneers made an impression on salute Khieu Samphan, Nuon Chea and Pol Pot on their "decisions" as President, President of the People's Representatives and Premier of Kampuchea, respectively. accordingly, in June 1976, the Kampuchean administration made an impression on the Provisional Revolutionary Government of the Republic of South Vietnam, which had administered South Vietnam since the fall of Saigon, complimenting them on the seventh commemoration of their establishment.

In July 1976, after the foundation of the Socialist Republic of Vietnam as a reunified nation, Phnom Penh Radio communicate a discourse which declared the "aggressor solidarity and kinship between people groups of Democratic Kampuchea and the Socialist Republic of Vietnam become continually greener and sturdier". However, during that equivalent month, Pol Pot freely alluded to pressures among Vietnam and Kampuchea when he told a meeting Vietnamese media designation that there were "snags and troubles" in the connection between the two countries. Nonetheless, on 21 September 1976, the primary air administration associating Hanoi and Ho Chi Minh City with Phnom Penh was set up. At that point in December 1976, the Kampuchean Revolutionary Organization sent welcome to the Vietnamese Communist Party during their Fourth Congress.

2.1 1977: build-up to war

Towards the finish of 1976, while Vietnam and Kampuchea openly gave off an impression of being improving their connections, the private doubts of the two nations' initiative developed. From the Vietnamese viewpoint, they were the benefactors of veritable Marxist–Leninist insurgencies in Southeast Asia, so it was indispensable for them to practice command over the Kampucheans and the Laotians. Indeed, that was the explanation North Vietnam supported the Khmer Rouge during their battle against the Lon Nol system, with the expectation that the Kampuchean socialists would embrace an ace Vietnamese line upon their victory similarly as the Pathet Lao had done. Be that as it may, their expectations were run as right on time as 1973, in light of the fact that People's Army of Vietnam (PAVN) developments working in Khmer Rouge-occupied territories were every so often exposed to outfitted assaults by their partners. The Vietnamese situation inside Kampuchea was additionally debilitated after the finish of the war, as there were no ace Vietnamese components left inside the Kampuchean Communist Party.

At the point when the star Chinese Pol Pot and his brother by marriage Ieng Sary left their individual situations as chief and outside pastor in September 1976, Vietnamese Prime Minister Phạm Văn Đồng and General Secretary of the Communist Party Lê Duẩn were idealistic that Vietnam could practice more prominent effect on the Kampucheans. In a private gathering with the Soviet minister to Vietnam on 16 November 1976, Lê Duẩn rejected both Ieng Sary and Pol Pot as "terrible individuals" for their expert Chinese policies. Le Duan then stated that Nuon Chea, who had rose to the situation of Premier of Democratic Kampuchea as Pol Pot's substitution, was an individual of genius Vietnamese direction, so Vietnam could practice its impact through him. In any case, the occasions which created throughout the following hardly any months would demonstrate Lê Duẩn had been mixed up in his evaluation of Nuon Chea.

In the interim, in Phnom Penh, the Kampuchean authority had built up a dread and contempt of the Vietnamese administration because of Vietnam's historical strength over their nation. From the Kampuchean point of view, the Vietnamese procedure to overwhelm Indochina included invading the socialist gatherings of Kampuchea and Laos with Vietnamese-prepared cadres. For that reason, when the primary group of North Vietnamese-prepared Khmer Rouge work force came back to the nation, they were quickly cleansed from the KCP. During the months following the annihilation of the Lon Nol system, Pol Pot kept on cleansing the KCP and the Government of Democratic Kampuchea of the individuals who he accepted to be Soviet and Vietnamese operators. At that point, with regards to the triumphalism that won among the Khmer Rouge administration—they guaranteed they had without any assistance vanquished the "American settlers"— Democratic Kampuchea started planning for war against Vietnam.

On 30 April 1977, the second commemoration of the fall of Saigon, the Kampuchean answer came as a military assault against the Vietnamese territories of A Giang and Châu Đốc, killing many Vietnamese civilians. The PAVN reacted by moving its soldiers to zones assaulted by Kampuchea and, on 7 June 1977, Vietnam proposed elevated level converses with talk about outstanding issues. On 18 June 1977, the Kampuchean Government answered by demanding that Vietnam evacuate the entirety of its military units from the contested territories, and make a neutral territory between the contradicting forces.

The two sides overlooked each other's recommendations, and the KRA kept sending troopers over the outskirt to assault Vietnamese towns and towns. In September 1977, KRA big guns struck a few Vietnamese towns along the outskirt, and six towns in Đồng Tháp Province were overwhelmed by Kampuchean infantry. Without further ado afterwards, six divisions of the KRA progressed around 10 kilometers (6.2 mi) into Tay Ninh Province, where they slaughtered in excess of 1,000 Vietnamese civilians. Angered by the size of Kampuchean attacks, the PAVN amassed eight divisions, assessed at around 60,000 fighters, to dispatch a retaliatory negative mark against Kampuchea. On 16 December 1977, the PAVN divisions, with support from components of the Vietnam People's Air Force, crossed the outskirt along a few tomahawks with the goal of compelling the Kampuchean Government to negotiate.

On the war zone, the KRA immediately lost ground to the Vietnamese. Before the finish of December 1977, Vietnam had prevailed upon a reasonable military victory Kampuchea, as Vietnamese arrangements walked through Svay Rieng Province and just stopped shy of entering the commonplace capital. Regardless of the savagery of the Vietnamese counter, the Kampuchean Government remained defiant. On 6 January 1978, PAVN divisions were just 38 kilometers (24 mi) from Phnom Penh, however the Vietnamese Government chose to pull back its powers from Kampuchea since they had neglected to accomplish Vietnam's political goal. During the withdrawal, the PAVN likewise cleared thousands of detainees and non military personnel outcasts, including future pioneer Hun Sen.

2.2 1978: arrangements for system change

Rather than being calmed by the Vietnamese demonstration of power, the Kampuchean government flaunted that the Vietnamese withdrawal was a significant victory for Democratic Kampuchea, contrasting it with the "annihilation of U.S. government" on 17 April 1975. The Kampucheans went on further to broadcast that "our 6 January victory over the annexationist, Vietnamese assailant foe has given we all more prominent trust in the powers of our kin and country, in our Kampuchean Communist Party and our Kampuchean Revolutionary Army, and in our Party's line of individuals' war". The Kampuchean initiative asserted that one Kampuchean officer was equivalent to 30 Vietnamese warriors, so if Kampuchea could raise 2,000,000 troopers from a populace of 8,000,000, it could crash Vietnam's populace of 50 million and still have 6,000,000 individuals left. as a general rule, Kampuchean pioneers basically overlooked the state of the populace in their own nation and Vietnam; the Vietnamese, however poor, were in great physical condition, while Kampuchea's populace was physically and rationally depleted from long periods of hard work, starvation and disease.

Notwithstanding the difference in populace, there was additionally an extraordinary dissimilarity between the battling abilities of the military of the two nations. In 1977, Vietnam was assessed to have 615,000 fighters and 900 tanks, supported by a 12,000-part aviation based armed forces with 300 battle flying machine, including one squadron of light aircraft. In correlation, Kampuchea had a multitude of 70,000, just a couple of substantial tanks, 200 defensively covered vehicles and constrained air capability. Despite confronting such overwhelming chances, Kampuchea gave no indications of faltering as its military kept on attacking Vietnam's outskirt districts. In January 1978, KRA powers still held segments of Vietnamese territory and started invading Vietnamese stations in Hà Tiên Province. On 27 January 1978, Vietnam began approaching the KRA along the fringe areas to topple the Khmer Rouge regime.

Against the scenery of military conflicts, between 9 January and 20 February 1978, Vietnamese Deputy Foreign Minister Phan Hien made a few outings to Beijing to have discourses with agents of the Kampuchean government, which at last demonstrated to be pointless. On 18 January 1978, China endeavored to intervene among Kampuchea and Vietnam when Vice Premier Deng Yingchao headed out to Phnom Penh, where she was met with solid obstruction by Kampuchean leaders. Meanwhile, Vietnamese government officials started directing mystery gatherings with So Phim, the Khmer Rouge pioneer in Kampuchea's Eastern Military Zone, to design a military uprising supported by Vietnam. During that equivalent period, military misfortunes experienced by the KRA in the Eastern Military Zone provoked Pol Pot to mark the area as a "home of traitors".

So as to cleanse the Eastern Military Zone of those he saw to have been sullied by the Vietnamese, Pol Pot requested military units from the Southwest Zone to move into eastern Kampuchea and dispose of the "shrouded traitors". Unfit to withstand an assault from the Kampuchea Government, So Phim ended it all while his agent Heng Samrin surrendered to Vietnam. On 12 April 1978, the Kampuchean government announced they and Vietnam could haggle again if the Vietnamese surrendered their expansionist desire and perceived Kampuchea's sovereignty. However, there was additionally a pre-condition expecting Vietnam to meet a few commitments through a seven-month preliminary truce. The Vietnamese government quickly dismissed the demand. Accordingly, two KRA divisions entered up to 2 kilometers (1.2 mi) into Vietnamese territory and slaughtered more than 3,000 Vietnamese regular citizens in the town of Ba Chúc in A Giang Province.

In June 1978, the VPAF began besieging KRA positions along the fringe locales, flying around 30 shelling forays for every day and delivering overwhelming setbacks on the Kampucheans. By that phase in the contention, most enduring pioneers of the Eastern Military Zone had gotten away into Vietnam, where they collected at different mystery camps to shape a Vietnamese-supported "freedom armed force" to battle against the Khmer Rouge regime. Meanwhile, the Vietnamese Communist Party Politburo was meeting in Hanoi to talk about its procedure for Kampuchea. It presumed that the Khmer Rouge system was an intermediary of China, which had been attempting to fill the power vacuum following the withdrawal of the United States. All things considered, China was distinguished as Vietnam's primary foe, and its customer system in Phnom Penh must be evacuated by traditional military power, in light of the fact that the Vietnamese adjustment of the Maoist "individuals' war" teaching had not been a triumph against the Khmer Rouge's security apparatus.

To mirror the frame of mind of the nation's heads, Vietnam's state-controlled media ventured up its propaganda war against the Khmer Rouge, with the official Nhân Dân paper normally calling for worldwide mediation to spare the Kampuchean individuals from residential fear started by the Khmer Rouge system. Besides, rather than sending congratulatory messages as they had done in the earlier years, the Vietnamese media changed their tone and started alluding to the Kampuchean Government as the "Pol Pot-Ieng Sary faction" as the Kampuchean military proceeded with their battle in Vietnam. By the finish of June, the Vietnamese military amassed a multi-division team to dispatch another constrained target crusade against the Kampucheans. Once more, the Vietnamese pushed the KRA powers once again into the commonplace urban communities of Suong and Prey Veng and then hauled out. Be that as it may, as they had done previously, the KRA moved its cannons back towards the outskirt and kept shelling Vietnamese towns as if nothing had happened.

During the second 50% of 1978, Vietnamese pioneers dedicated quite a bit of their vitality towards the military crusade against the Khmer Rouge system, by looking for political support from the Soviet Union. In a preparation with Vietnamese Foreign Ministry officials on 25 July 1978, the Soviet chargé d'affaires in Hanoi was told that the Kampuchean Government had conveyed 14 of its 17 standard armed force divisions and 16 neighborhood regiments along the outskirt with Vietnam. While Vietnam was establishing the political framework for the military crusade against Kampuchea, Soviet boats were accounted for to empty military hardware and ammo in Cam Ranh Bay. In October 1978, Vietnamese radio station what they asserted were records of uprisings against the Khmer Rouge system, encouraging individuals from the KRA either to topple the "Pol Pot-Ieng Sary coterie" or deformity to

Vietnam.

In a significant defining moment over the span of Soviet-Vietnamese and Sino-Vietnamese discretionary relations, and at last the Vietnamese intrusion of Kampuchea, a Treaty of Friendship and Cooperation was marked among Vietnam and the Soviet Union on 3 November 1978, which ensured the previous of imperative Soviet military guide in the situation that China mediated in the conflict. Later, in November 1978, a command and control home office was built up for the arranged attack of Kampuchea, with Senior General Lê Đức Anh assuming full responsibility for PAVN units along the outskirt territories. The Vietnamese government drafted 350,000 men into the military to supplant prior misfortunes and expand its units along the outskirt. While the newcomers were finishing preparing, ten divisions were sent to the outskirt locales of Long A, Đồng Tháp and Tây Ninh Provinces. Vietnam likewise moved three divisions situated in Laos south towards the Laos-Kampuchea border. On 13 December 1978, the Chinese Government warned Vietnam that its understanding was restricted, and that Vietnam would be rebuffed in the event that it carried on in an "unbridled fashion".

In any case, the last bit of the Vietnamese technique developed when Vietnam declared the arrangement of the Kampuchean United Front for National Salvation (KUFNS) in the "freedom zones" of Kampuchea. Hanoi guaranteed that KUFNS was an autonomous Kampuchean socialist development, with individuals drawn from varying backgrounds. Heng Samrin, some time ago an individual from the Khmer Rouge and commander of the KRA fourth Division, was the executive of the KUFNS Central Committee. Previously, the KUFNS was known as the Provisional Revolutionary Government of Kampuchea (PRGK), which comprised of 300 previous Khmer Rouge frameworks who abandoned to Vietnam. The PRGK consistently sent agents to another country looking for support, before Vietnam abandoned the "individuals' war" idea for a traditional military campaign.

Not to be beaten by the Vietnamese military build-up, the Government of Democratic Kampuchea was caught up with fortifying its military with Chinese support. In earlier years, China had just given the KRA a restricted amounts of arms and ammo, yet as relations with Vietnam intensified in

1978, Beijing built up extra supply courses through Kampuchea and expanded the volume of military hardware which went down each route. On the eve of the Vietnamese attack, Kampuchea had an expected 73,000 warriors in the Eastern Military Zone flanking Vietnam. around then, all parts of the Kampuchean military were altogether fortified by huge amounts of Chinese-made military gear, which included contender flying machine, watch vessels, overwhelming big guns, against air ship weapons, trucks and tanks. Also, there were somewhere in the range of 10,000 and 20,000 Chinese consultants in both military and non military personnel limits, giving their support to the Khmer Rouge regime.

Chapter 3 : Invasion of Kampuchea

On 21 December 1978, Kampuchea's freshly discovered quality was tried when a Vietnamese offensive, comprising of two divisions, crossed the fringe and moved towards the town of Kratie, while other support divisions were conveyed along neighborhood courses to remove the strategic tail of Kampuchean units. Despite getting a charge out of liberal support from China, the KRA couldn't withstand the Vietnamese offensive and endured substantial casualties. Finally, on 25 December 1978, Vietnam propelled a full-scale intrusion utilizing 13 divisions, assessed at 150,000 warriors well-supported by overwhelming cannons and air power. Initially, Kampuchea legitimately tested Vietnam's military may through ordinary battling techniques, however this strategy brought about the loss of half of the KRA inside about fourteen days. Substantial thrashings on the war zone provoked a significant part of the Kampuchean authority to clear towards the western locale of the country. On 7 January 1979, the PAVN entered Phnom Penh alongside individuals from the KUFNS. On the next day, an expert Vietnamese Kampuchean state, known as the People's Republic of Kampuchea (PRK), was set up, with Heng Samrin as the Chief of State and Pen Sovan as General Secretary of the recently refounded Kampuchean People's Revolutionary Party.

The Khmer Rouge initiative, with quite a bit of its political and military structures broke by the Vietnamese intrusion, had to take asylum in Thailand, where it was warmly invited by the Thai Government. In spite of the mind-boggling monetary difficulties brought by the Khmer Rouge and the going with evacuees, the Thai Government shielded and ensured the Khmer Rouge at Khao Larn camp in Trat Province. Meanwhile, in Phnom Penh, the new Kampuchean system attempted to rebuild the nation's financial and public activity, which was to a great extent wrecked by many years of political upheavals and steady warfare. Notwithstanding, endeavors to rebuild the nation were seriously hampered by the absence of taught and qualified work force, as most instructed individuals had either fled the nation or had been killed by the Khmer Rouge system during the past four years. Before the year's over, the new system's endeavors at country building were additionally tested by a few enemy of Vietnamese obstruction groups working in the western areas of the country.

3.1 International response

Not long after the catch of Phnom Penh, delegates of Democratic Kampuchea required a crisis meeting of the United Nations Security Council, so Prince Sihanouk could introduce the dismissed system's case. In spite of solid protests from the Soviet Union and Czechoslovakia, the UN Security Council gave Sihanouk this chance. Although Sihanouk separated himself from the human rights maltreatment of the Khmer Rouge, he blamed Vietnam for utilizing animosity to abuse Kampuchea's sway. All things considered, he demanded all UN nations suspend help to Vietnam and not perceive the Vietnamese-introduced regime. Subsequently, seven uncommitted individuals from the UN Security Council presented a draft goals requiring a truce and the withdrawal of every single remote power from Kampuchea, which was embraced by China, France, Norway, Portugal, the United States and the United Kingdom. Be that as it may, the goals was not affirmed because of restriction from the Soviet Union and Czechoslovakia. Ted Galen Carpenter, an international strategy investigator from the Cato Institute, contends that Vietnam didn't attack Cambodia out of any respectable want to stop the abominations submitted by Pol Pot's system but instead to combine their control of Indochina.

Between 16–19 February 1979 Vietnam and the new Kampuchean system held a summit meeting which closed with the two nations marking a Treaty of Peace, Friendship and Cooperation. Article 2 of the arrangement expressed that the security of Vietnam and Kampuchea were interrelated; in this way they would help guard each other "against plans and demonstrations of treachery by the radical and worldwide reactionary powers", along these lines legitimizing the nearness of Vietnamese soldiers on Kampuchean soil. Soon afterwards, the Soviet Union, the communist nations of Eastern Europe and India perceived the Vietnamese-introduced People's Republic of Kampuchea. The Soviet government lauded the PRK's "surprising victory" and communicated its full support for the system's development towards communism. Moreover, the Soviets brutally censured the Khmer Rouge system's record of fear, which they suggested had been forced by China.

At the 34th Session of the UN General Assembly, agents of the People's Republic of Kampuchea and Democratic Kampuchea both asserted the privilege to speak to their nation. The previous likewise advised the part countries of the UN Security Council that it was the sole real delegate of Kampuchea and its people. accordingly, the UN Credentials Committee chose to perceive Democratic Kampuchea by a vote of six to three, in spite of the Khmer Rouge's blood-recolored record while in control. In like manner, delegates of Democratic Kampuchea were permitted to be situated in the General Assembly, with solid support from China. By January 1980, 29 nations had built up conciliatory relations with the People's Republic of Kampuchea, yet almost 80 nations still perceived the authenticity of the dismissed Democratic Kampuchea. Simultaneously, the Western forces and the part nations of the Association of Southeast Asian Nations (ASEAN) additionally voiced solid judgment of Vietnam's utilization of power to evacuate the Khmer Rouge regime.

Thailand, which shared a 800-kilometer (500 mile) fringe with Kampuchea and has historically dreaded Vietnam's expansionism, demanded that Vietnam quickly expel its soldiers from Kampuchea so its kin could choose an administration liberated from remote mediation. Indonesia, Malaysia, the Philippines and Singapore indicated their support for Thailand's position. Furthermore, ASEAN saw Vietnam's intrusion and resulting occupation of Kampuchea, which got solid Soviet support, as an intolerable danger to the district's security and stability. That view was shared by China, which went the extent that blaming Vietnam for constraining Kampuchea into an

Indochinese organization to fill in as a station of Soviet worldwide authority.

The United States, which never kept up any type of political ties with the Khmer Rouge's Democratic Kampuchea, indicated solid support for the participation of their previous adversary in the UN General Assembly, and reverberated ASEAN's require a prompt withdrawal of Vietnamese military powers from Kampuchea.

Likewise, North Korea, whose pioneer Kim Il-sung had offered Sihanouk asylum after he was expelled by Lon Nol in 1970, additionally would not perceive the People's Republic of Kampuchea.

3.2 China attacks Vietnam

On 17 February 1979, China attacked Vietnam, meaning to catching the capitals of its outskirt areas so as to drive a Vietnamese withdrawal from Cambodia. The intrusion was impeded by obstruction from nearby civilian armies and some ordinary armed force fortifications; by the by, the Chinese armed force caught Cao Bằng and Lao Cai following three weeks and Lạng Sơn following a month. The next day, China declared that it would not move further into Vietnam, evidently subsequent to meeting out of the blue cruel opposition by well-prepared Vietnamese powers outfitted with Soviet and caught American weapons. Besides, Vietnam's politburo had requested a general assembly and started getting ready for full enrollment. The Chinese thusly pulled back their forces. Although China bombed either to conclusively win the multi day struggle or to compel a withdrawal of Vietnamese powers in Cambodia, the preoccupation of troops from Kampuchea encouraged a resurgence in Khmer Rouge extremist tasks, making it unavoidable for the youthful PRK system in Kampuchea to execute conscription. China's positioning of a huge power on the outskirt and taking part in fringe engagements during resulting clashes likewise expected Vietnam to station a huge segment of its military along the Sino-Vietnamese outskirt all through the 1980s.

Chapter 4: KPNLF insurgency

At the point when the Khmer Rouge system was expelled from control in January 1979, the Kampuchean individuals trusted that harmony and freedom would come back to their nation. This was fortified by the Constitution of the People's Republic of Kampuchea, announced in 1981, which explicitly expressed that Kampuchea was an autonomous, serene state where power had a place with the people. However, there was a profound differentiation between what was written in the constitution and reality, in light of the fact that the Kampuchean individuals started to surrender at what they saw as the Vietnamese occupation of their nation, instead of a freedom that had liberated them from the fierceness of Democratic Kampuchea. That discernment was strengthened by the nearness of Vietnamese counselors who worked at each degree of Heng Samrin's Kampuchean Government. In 1986, for instance, there was one Vietnamese consultant for each Kampuchean bureau pastor and one counselor for every single one of their three appointee clergymen. Moreover, it was accounted for that official conclusions made by a Kampuchean priest needed to get last endorsement from the Vietnamese counselor, who generally directed policies. Opposition to the Vietnamese was additionally instigated by human rights manhandles submitted by the Vietnamese and their partners. To satisfy its K5 Plan, a development venture to fortify the Cambodia-Thai fringe, the PRK government recruited 380,000 individuals, with huge numbers surrendering to malaria. Claude Malhuret of Médecins Sans Frontières revealed that a strategy the Vietnamese and KPRAF used to battle the Khmer Rouge was to retain nourishment from regions constrained by the Khmer Rouge. Thousands of tons of nourishment gave by global help associations ruined on the docks of Kompong Som. Nourishment sent by help associations was often rather used to encourage Vietnamese soldiers and Cambodians living under Vietnamese control.

To oppose the Vietnamese occupation of Kampuchea and the system which they introduced, the Khmer Rouge approached the Kampuchean individuals to join together and battle the Vietnamese. Be that as it may, because of the severity which they had encountered under the removed system, numerous Kampucheans accepted that any political development planned for restoring national opportunity must restrict both the Khmer Rouge and the Vietnamese.

in light of such preconditions, two non-socialist developments were shaped to battle the Vietnamese occupation. The primary group, a conservative and professional Western association, was framed in October 1979 by previous Prime Minister Son Sann and was known as the Khmer People's National Liberation Front (KPNLF). The KPNLF worked from a few displaced person camps on the Thai-Cambodian outskirt, where it controlled thousands of civilians. At its pinnacle, the outfitted part of the KPNLF were assessed to have somewhere in the range of 12,000 and 15,000 contenders, yet 33% of that number were lost through battling and departures during the Vietnamese dry season offensive of 1984–1985. In any case, the KPNLF kept on working in little groups, bothering the Vietnamese and their Kampuchean partners utilizing guerrilla tactics.

The other non-socialist association was the National United Front for an Independent, Peaceful, Neutral, and Cooperative Cambodia, framed by Sihanouk and known by its French abbreviation FUNCINPEC. The association was shaped after Sihanouk had disavowed the Khmer Rouge following his portrayal for its benefit at the UN Security Council. As the pioneer of FUNCINPEC, Sihanouk approached the UN General Assembly to oust Khmer Rouge agents for their violations while in control and to keep Kampuchea's seat at the UN empty on the premise that neither the Khmer Rouge nor the Vietnamese-introduced PRK had the mandate to speak to the Kampuchean people. He additionally censured ASEAN for its proceeded with acknowledgment of the Khmer Rouge, and explicitly Thailand for empowering Chinese arms shipments to make a trip through its territory to supply the notorious socialist group. In spite of the quality, adequacy and prevalence of the KPNLF and the FUNCINPEC, both opposition groups were tormented by inward divisions brought about by the absence of solidarity, administration battles, corruption and affirmed maltreatment of human rights.

In the beginning of the Vietnamese occupation, Kampuchean opposition groups had constrained contact with one another because of their disparities. Despite the fact that the Khmer Rouge delighted in across the board global acknowledgment, by 1980 the association was feeling the squeeze from the universal network to change itself. ASEAN, which had sponsored the Khmer

Rouge all through their discretionary encounters with the PRK system at the UN General Assembly in 1979, encouraged the Khmer Rouge authority to take care of its blood-recolored picture behind it to unite with other non-socialist movements. framing a partnership with the Khmer Rouge at first caused a specific level of uneasiness inside the administration circles of the FUNCINPEC and the KPNLF, in light of the fact that the two groups were cautious about getting together with a socialist association surely understood for its fierceness. Regardless, from the get-go in 1981, Sihanouk and Son Sann started participating in converses with Khieu Samphan, President of the removed Democratic Kampuchea, to examine the possibility of shaping an alliance.

In August 1981, solidarity talks between the three associations seemed to have crumpled because of clashing interests. Sihanouk, who dreaded the resurgence of the Khmer Rouge, suggested that all opposition groups incapacitate themselves following the withdrawal of Vietnamese soldiers from Kampuchea. In the interim, Son Sann demanded that the KPNLF be the lead association inside the proposed partnership, and the pioneers of the Khmer Rouge "most undermined" by the barbarities in Kampuchea be ousted to China. Against these preconditions, Khieu Samphan reminded his opponents that the autonomy of the Khmer Rouge and Democratic Kampuchea ought not be undermined. On 22 November 1982, Singapore, with the sponsorship of ASEAN, suggested that three associations structure an alliance government with equivalent basic leadership controls inside the union. Singapore's proposition was invited by Sihanouk, who trusted it was a reasonable arrangement for the non-socialist movements. Khieu Samphan, then again, dismissed that thought, seeing it as an endeavor by Sihanouk and Son Sann to separate the Khmer Rouge. Notwithstanding, Sihanouk realized that Chinese support would not be made accessible to the FUNCINPEC except if he made a few trade offs and joined the Khmer Rouge on their terms. So, in February 1982, Sihanouk met with Khieu Samphan in Beijing to work out their disparities. In what he depicted as "another concession", Khieu Samphan proposed framing an alliance government without incorporating the other obstruction groups into organizations related with Democratic Kampuchea. In any case, he stressed that all gatherings must safeguard the lawful status of Democratic Kampuchea as the authentic state speaking to Kampuchea on the world stage. In May 1982, with the asking of Sihanouk,

Son Sann chose to frame an alliance government with the Khmer Rouge.

On 22 June 1982, pioneers of the three associations formalized the arrangement of their alliance government by consenting to a Thai-supported arrangement which set up the Coalition Government of Democratic Kampuchea (CGDK). In like manner, the CGDK's Inner Cabinet comprised of Sihanouk as the President of Democratic Kampuchea, Khieu Samphan as the Vice-President responsible for remote issues and Son Sann as Prime Minister. Beneath the Inner Cabinet were six separate boards of trustees answerable for national barrier, economy and fund, parties and general wellbeing, military undertakings and the media. During a gathering between Kim Il-sung and Sihanouk on 10 April 1986, in Pyongyang, Kim Il-Sung consoled Sihanouk that North Korea would keep on viewing him as the real head of province of Kampuchea. By 1987, Democratic Kampuchea still held its participation at the UN General Assembly, despite the fact that it needed four criteria of statehood: individuals, territory, government, and supreme authority inside the outskirts of a country. disregarding those constraints, powers of the three equipped factions inside the CGDK kept on battling the Vietnamese to accomplish their goal of "bringing about the execution of the International Conference on Cambodia and other pertinent UN General Assembly resolutions".

Chapter 5 : Vietnamese reform and withdrawal

At the point when the Vietnamese heads propelled their intrusion of Kampuchea to expel the Khmer Rouge system in 1978, they didn't anticipate a negative reaction from the worldwide network. Be that as it may, the occasions that pursued the attack demonstrated that they had seriously misjudged worldwide feelings for their motivation. Rather than sponsorship Vietnam, most United Nations part nations impugned the Vietnamese utilization of power against Kampuchea, and even moved to restore the battered Khmer Rouge association that had once represented the nation with such brutality. Thus, Kampuchea turned out to be something other than a military issue for Vietnam, rapidly developing into a financial and strategic issue in the worldwide field. During the time where Vietnam occupied neighboring Kampuchea, the Vietnamese Government, and the PRK system which it introduced, were put on the outskirts of the global community.

The global network's political position towards Kampuchea severy affected the Vietnamese economy, which was at that point destroyed by many years of ceaseless clashes. The United States, which previously had authorizes set up against Vietnam, persuaded different nations of the United Nations to deny Vietnam and the People's Republic of Kampuchea of much-required assets by denying them participation to significant universal associations, for example, the World Bank, the Asian Development Bank and the International Monetary Fund. In 1979 Japan ventured up the weight by suspending all financial guide to Vietnam, and warned Vietnamese pioneers that financial guide would possibly continue when Vietnam altered its approaches towards Kampuchea, the Sino-Soviet competition and the issue of the vessel people. Sweden, which was viewed as the staunchest supporter of Vietnam in the West, additionally considered decreasing its duties to the socialist nation as practically every other nation dropped its aid.

Notwithstanding outer weight, local strategies actualized by the Vietnamese Government since 1975 had demonstrated to be to a great extent inadequate in animating the nation's financial development. By building on the Soviet model of focal financial arranging, Vietnam set most accentuation on the improvement of substantial businesses, while generation in farming and light assembling sectors stagnated. Furthermore, endeavors to nationalize the economy of southern Vietnam after reunification just brought about disorder, as monetary yield was driven somewhere near separation of the all inclusive community. Notwithstanding those bombed financial strategies, Vietnam kept up the fifth-biggest military on the planet, with 1.26 million ordinary officers under arms, 180,000 of whom were positioned in Cambodia in 1984. Consequently, the Vietnamese Government needed to burn through 33% of its spending limit on the military and the crusade in Kampuchea, regardless of accepting US$1.2 billion in military guide yearly from the Soviet Union, in this manner further hampering Vietnam's monetary rebuilding efforts.

In light of worldwide weight, and to abstain from participating in a crippling clash with different neighborhood furnished opposition groups, Vietnam started pulling back its military powers from Kampuchea as right on time as 1982. In any case, the withdrawal procedure needed worldwide confirmation, so remote spectators just expelled Vietnam's development of troops as unimportant rotations. In 1984, so as to separate from Kampuchea, Vietnam uncovered a five-stage methodology known as the K5 Plan. The arrangement was composed by General Le Duc Anh, who had driven the Vietnamese battle in Kampuchea. The primary stage required the Vietnamese military to catch the bases of equipped groups in western Kampuchea and along the outskirt with Thailand. The accompanying stages included close the fringe with Thailand, crushing nearby opposition groups, giving security to the populace, and building up the Kampuchean People's Revolutionary Armed Forces. Foreign spectators accepted that the Vietnamese Army finished the primary period of the K5 Plan during the dry season offensive of 1984–85, when the base camps of a few enemy of Vietnamese obstruction groups were invaded. Afterwards, most of ten Vietnamese divisions were doled out to activities on the wildernesses, with the rest of in significant territories to secure the neighborhood populace and to prepare the Kampuchean military.

By 1985, worldwide disengagement and financial hardships had constrained Vietnam to depend increasingly more on the Soviet Union for help. During the Chinese attack in February 1979, the Soviet Union gave US$1.4 billion worth of military guide to Vietnam, a figure that crested at US$1.7 billion in the period somewhere in the range of 1981 and 1985. Then, to assist Vietnam with actualizing its third Five Year Plan, the Soviet Union gave a whole of US$5.4 billion to the Vietnamese Government for its uses; monetary guide at last came to US$1.8 billion every year. The Soviet Union likewise gave 90% of Vietnam's demand to crude materials and 70% of its grain imports. Even however the figures propose the Soviet Union was a dependable partner, secretly Soviet pioneers were disappointed with Hanoi's handling of the impasse in Kampuchea and disliked the weight of their guide program to Vietnam as their own nation was experiencing financial reforms. In 1986, the Soviet Government declared that it would lessen help to agreeable countries; for Vietnam, those decreases implied the loss of 20% of its monetary guide and 33% of its military guide.

To reconnect with the global network, and to manage the monetary difficulties brought by the adjustments in the Soviet Union and Eastern Europe, Vietnamese pioneers chose to set out on a progression of changes. At the sixth National Party Congress in December 1986, recently selected General Secretary of the VCP Nguyen Van Linh presented a significant change known as Đổi Mới, the Vietnamese expression for "redesign", so as to fix Vietnam's financial problems. However, Vietnamese pioneers inferred that Vietnam's critical monetary circumstance came because of the worldwide detachment which pursued its intrusion of Kampuchea in 1978, and that for Đổi Mới to be effective it required radical changes in protection and outside policy. Subsequently, in June 1987, the Vietnamese Politburo received another barrier technique in Resolution No. 2, requiring the total withdrawal of Vietnamese troopers from universal obligations, a decrease in the size of the military through a release of 600,000 officers and the foundation of a set proportion for military expenditures.

At that point, on 13 May 1988, the Vietnamese Politburo embraced Resolution No. 13 on international strategy, which expected to accomplish expansion and multilateralisation of Vietnam's outside relations. Its principle targets were to end the embargoes forced by UN individuals, incorporate Vietnam with the territorial and worldwide network, and eventually pull in remote venture and advancement aid. As a major aspect of this change, Vietnam stopped to see the United States as a long haul adversary and China as an inevitable and risky foe. What's more, official Vietnamese propaganda stopped marking ASEAN as a "NATO-type" organisation. To execute the new changes, Vietnam, with support from the Soviet Union, began moving quite a long while of military gear to the KPRAF, which numbered in excess of 70,000 troopers. The Vietnamese Ministry of Defense's International

Relations Department at that point exhorted its Kampuchean partners to just utilize the accessible hardware to keep up their present degree of tasks, and not to participate in significant activities which could deplete those supplies.

In 1988, Vietnam was assessed to have around 100,000 soldiers in Kampuchea, at the same time, detecting that a political settlement was inside come to, the Vietnamese Government started pulling back powers decisively. Among April and July 1989, 24,000 Vietnamese troopers came all the way back. At that point, somewhere in the range of 21 and 26 September 1989, in the wake of enduring 15,000 warriors slaughtered and another 30,000 injured during the 10-year occupation, Vietnam's pledge to Kampuchea was officially finished, when the staying 26,000 Vietnamese fighters were pulled out.

However, outfitted obstruction groups contradicted to the Vietnamese-introduced PRK system asserted that Vietnamese soldiers were all the while working on Kampuchean soil long after September 1989. For instance, non-socialist groups taking part in land-get activities in western Kampuchea after the withdrawal detailed conflicts with tip top Vietnamese Special Forces close Tamar Puok along Route 69. Then, in March 1991, Vietnamese units were accounted for to have reemerged Kampot Province to overcome a Khmer Rouge offensive. Despite such claims, on 23 October 1991, the Vietnamese Government consented to the Paris Peace Arrangement, which planned to restore harmony in Kampuchea.

Chapter 6 : United Front for the Liberation of Oppressed Races

The United Front for the Liberation of Oppressed Races was an association in Vietnam whose goal was autonomy for the Degar (Montagnard) clans. At first a political patriot development, after 1969 it advanced into a divided guerrilla group that carried on revolts against, progressively, the legislatures of South Vietnam and the Socialist Republic of Vietnam. Restricted to all types of Vietnamese principle, FULRO battled against the socialist Viet Cong and entrepreneur ARVN simultaneously. FULRO's essential supporter was Cambodia, with some guide sent by China.

On May 1, 1958, a group of scholarly people headed by a French-taught Rhade government worker, Y Bham Enuol, built up an association looking for more noteworthy autonomy for the minorities of the Vietnamese Central Highlands. The association was given the name BAJARAKA, which stood for four primary ethnic groups: the Bahnar individuals, the Jarai (Gia Rai individuals), the Rhade or E De individuals, and the K'Ho individuals.

On July 25, BAJARAKA gave a notification to the international safe havens of France and the United States and to the United Nations, condemning demonstrations of racial separation, and mentioning government mediation to verify freedom. In August–September 1958, BAJARAKA held a few exhibits in Kon Tum, Pleiku, and Buôn Ma Thuột. These were immediately suppressed, and the most conspicuous pioneers of the development captured: they would stay in prison for the following hardly any years.

One of BAJARAKA's pioneers, Y Bih Aleo, later joined the National Liberation Front of South Vietnam, all the more generally known as the Viet Cong.

6.1 The FLHP

The mid 1960s were to see expanding military action in the Central Highlands; from 1961, American military guides had helped with setting up furnished town resistance state armies (the Civilian Irregular Defense Groups, CIDG).

In 1963, after the 1963 South Vietnamese coup to topple Ngô Đình Diệm, every one of the pioneers of BAJARAKA were discharged. With an end goal to incorporate Degar desire, a few of them were given government posts: Paul Nur, VP of BAJARAKA, was selected representative commonplace boss for the area of Kon Tum, while Y Bham Enuol, the development's leader, was delegated appointee common legislative head of Đăk Lăk Province. By March 1964, with US backing, the pioneers of BAJARAKA, alongside delegates of other ethnic groups and of the Upper Cham individuals, built up the Central Highlands Liberation Front (French: Front de Liberation des Hauts Plateaux, FLHP).

The Front quickly split into two factions. One faction, pushing serene methods, was driven by Y Bham Enuol. A second, drove by Y Dhơn Adrong, supported fierce obstruction. From March to May 1964, Adrong's faction invaded the fringe with Cambodia and set up at the old French base, Camp le Rolland, in Mondulkiri Province inside 15 km of the Vietnamese outskirt, where they kept on enlisting FLHP contenders.

6.2 FULRO

Meanwhile, the local aspirations of Cambodian Head of State, Prince Norodom Sihanouk, had prompted a push to arrange the tasks of different nonconformist groups working inside South Vietnam and in the Cambodian fringe regions. Contact was made between Adrong's faction of the FLHP and two different groups:

•   The Front for the Liberation of Champa (Front pour la Libération du Champa, FLC) drove by Lieutenant-Colonel Les Kosem, a Cham officer in the Royal Cambodian Army (FARK).

•   The Liberation Front of Kampuchea Krom (Front de Liberation du Kampuchea Krom, FLKK), speaking to the Khmer Krom of the Mekong Delta, drove by previous priest Chau Dara.

Kosem, the most senior Cham officer in the Cambodian armed force, had been associated with Cham activism since the late 1950s, and is suspected to have been filling in as a twofold operator for both the Cambodian mystery administration and the French. The FLKK, then again, started in a semi-spiritualist, semi-military group known as the "White Scarves" (Kaingsaing Sar) situated in the Seven Mountains region (Bảy Núi) of A Giang Province and established in the late 1950s by a priest, Samouk Seng (or Samouk Sen); this had been supported by Sihanouk as an offset to a republican guerrilla development working a similar zone, the Khmer Serei. Chau Dara was likewise suspected to be working for the Cambodian mystery service.

These contacts were to prompt the foundation of the United Front for the

Liberation of Oppressed Races (FULRO), in light of the above groups and the FLHP. The banner of FULRO was planned with three stripes: one blue (speaking to the ocean), red (an image of battle) and green (the shade of the mountains). Three white stars on the focal red stripe spoke to the three fronts of FULRO. A later type of the banner supplanted the blue stripe with dark.

6.3 The 1964 Buôn Ma Thuột rebellion

A few Vietnamese troopers were murdered and the Americans incapacitated, and FULRO activists from the Buon Sar Pa base held onto the radio broadcast on Route 14 on the south-west edges of Buôn Ma Thuột, from which they communicate calls for autonomy.

Untouchables prompting and helping the nonconformist Montagnard was Y-Dhon Adrong, an Ede (Rhade) ex-teacher, two officers of the Royal Khmer Army, Lieutenant Colonel Y-Bun Sur, an individual from the M'nong clan and Province Chief of Cambodia's Mondulkiri Province, and Lieutenant Colonel Les Kosem, a Cham. Another consultant was Chau Dara, a Cham who was ex-priest from South Vietnam's Mekong Delta.

On the night of September 21, 1964, Brigadier General Nguyễn Huu Co, the commander of Military Region II, who had flown down to Buôn Ma Thuột from his home office in Pleiku, met with a few renegade pioneers From Buon Enao during which he guaranteed them of his incomplete support of a portion of their demands in portrayals to Prime Minister General Nguyễn Khánh and the Saigon government. Following satisfactory exchanges, General Co mentioned that the revolutionary chiefs brief the other nonconformist components and ask them to calmly come back to their bases and anticipate the result of the arrangements. The pioneers who had met with General Co the earlier night were kept from instructions the Buon Sar Pa group which, still disappointed, came back to their Buon Sar Pa Special Forces base, joined by Colonel John F. Freund, the US Army guide to General Co. Colonel Freund's choice to go with the still protester Buon Sar Pa group was not approved by General Co.

The Buon Sar Pa group kept on challenging the Vietnamese specialists and a large portion of the CIDG power betrayed their Buon Sar Pa base and moved, with their weapons and gear over the universal fringe and into Cambodia's Mondulkiri Province. Those CIDG troops staying in the Buon Sar Pa base were compromised by General Co with a sharp military reaction and Colonel Freund, who had remained with them, convinced them to officially give up to

Prime Minister General Nguyễn Khánh. An official give up function took place in the for the most part abandoned Buon Sar Pa base in any case, this brought about lost face for those protester Montagnard who had consented to stand down and anticipate the guarantees made by General Co during dealings with their pioneers the evening of September 21, 1964.

Y-Bham was named head of FULRO and given the position of general and named President of the High Plateau of Champa, an indication of the impact on the dissenter Montagnard by the Cham guides, Lieutenant Colonel Les Kosem and Chau Dara.

A little while later, Y-Bham's family were discreetly taken from his town, Buon Ea Bong, three kilometers north-west of Buôn Ma Thuột and accompanied into the FULRO base in Cambodia's Mondulkiri Province.

Too, Colonel Y-Bun Sur was as yet the Province Chief of Cambodia's Mondulkiri Province. This demonstrates the probable inclusion of the administration of Prince Norodom Sihanouk. Colonel Y-Bun Sur was additionally an operator in France's mystery insight administration around then, the Service de Documentation Extérieure et de Contre-Espionnage (SDECE). This shows conceivable association of the French in the revolt.

The Americans were uncertain who was eventually liable for the CIDG men's resistance, and they at first accused the Viet Cong and French. However, the 'neutralist' Cambodian system of Sihanouk had presumably the best hand in occasions: 20 September 1964 'Presentation', by the Haut Comité of FULRO, contained enemy of SEATO rhetoric that drag a solid similarity to that gave by Sihanouk's system in the equivalent period. Sihanouk facilitated a gathering, the "Indochinese People's Conference", in Phnom Penh in mid 1965, at which Enuol headed a FULRO assignment.

Absence of progress in picking up concessions prompted another FULRO uprising by its increasingly aggressor faction in December 1965, in which 35 Vietnamese (counting regular citizens) were murdered. This occasion was quickly suppressed, and four caught FULRO commanders (Nay Re, Ksor Bleo, R'Com Re and Ksor Boh) were openly executed.

6.4 Negotiations and divisions

On June 2, 1967, Y Bham Enuol sent an assignment to Buôn Ma Thuột to appeal to the South Vietnamese government. On 25 and 26 June 1967, a congress of ethnic minorities all through South Vietnam was met to settle a joint appeal, and on August 29, 1967, a gathering was held under the bearing of Nguyễn Văn Thiệu, President of the National Leadership Committee and Major General Nguyen Cao Ky, President of the Central Executive Committee. By December 11, 1968, dealings among FULRO and the Vietnamese specialists had brought about a consent to perceive minority rights, set up a Ministry to support these rights, and to permit Y Bham Enuol to remain for all time in Vietnam.

In any case, a few components of FULRO, outstandingly the FLC head Les Kosem, contradicted the arrangement with the Vietnamese. On December 30, 1968, Kosem, at the leader of a few contingents of the Royal Cambodian Army, and joined by a group from the activist FULRO wing answerable for the 1965 battling, encompassed and took Camp le Rolland. Enuol was set under powerful house capture in Phnom Penh at the habitation of Colonel Um Savuth of the Cambodian armed force, where he was to stay for the following six years.

On February 1, 1969, a last bargain was marked between Paul Nur, speaking to the Republic of Vietnam, and Y Dhơn Adrong. These occasions implied the finish of FULRO as a 'political' development, particularly as its past patron, the Sangkum system of Sihanouk, was to tumble to the Cambodian coup of 1970. Be that as it may, a few components of FULRO, disappointed with the arrangement, proceeded with outfitted opposition in the Central Highlands. These different furnished groups anticipated the breakdown of the Saigon system, and had some neighborhood collaboration with the Viet Cong, who offered unofficial support, for example, thinking about their wounded.

In the wake of ousting master China Sihanouk, Cambodian pioneer Lon Nol, notwithstanding being enemy of Communist and apparently in the "ace American" camp, supported FULRO against all Vietnamese, both enemy of socialist South Vietnam and the Communist Viet Cong. Lon Nol arranged a butcher of all Vietnamese in Cambodia and a restoration of South Vietnam to a resuscitated Champa state.

Vietnamese were butchered and dumped in the Mekong River at the hands of Lon Nol's enemy of Communist forces. The Khmer Rouge later imitated Lon Nol's actions.

6.5 After the fall of South Vietnam

On April 17, 1975, the Cambodian Civil War finished when the Khmer Rouge socialists – at that point in a political collusion with Sihanouk, the GRUNK – took Phnom Penh. General Y Bham Enuol, Lieutenant Colonel Y-Bun Sur, and about 150 individuals from the activist FULRO faction were, at the time, under house capture in the compound of Colonel Um Savuth of the Khmer Army situated close Pochentong Airport. They left the compound and looked for asylum in the French Embassy. The Khmer Rouge constrained the senior French representative to hand the group, men ladies and youngsters, over to them. They were then walked to the Lambert Stadium then on the northern edge of Phnom Penh where they were executed by the Khmer Rouge alongside numerous officials of the Cambodian system; the remaining FULRO guerrillas in Vietnam, in any case, were to stay unaware of Enuol's passing.

After the Fall of Saigon and the breakdown of the South Vietnam government, it was recommended that the United States keep on supporting FULRO in its battle against the legislature of the Socialist Republic of Vietnam. A few thousand FULRO troops under Brigadier General Y-Ghok Niê Krieng continued battling Vietnamese powers, yet the guaranteed American guide didn't emerge.

FULRO proceeded with tasks in the remote highlands all through the late 1970s and into the mid 1980s, yet it was progressively debilitated by interior divisions, and caught in a continuous clash between the Khmer Rouge and Vietnamese. Despite this, in the mid 1980s there was a top in this second period of the FULRO uprising, potentially with dynamic material support from China, who profited by the contention as a major aspect of its progressing standoff with Vietnam. Some assessments gave the total number of FULRO troops in this period at 7,000, for the most part situated in Mondulkiri, and supplied with Chinese deadly implements by means of the Khmer Rouge, which was by this point battling its very own guerrilla war in western Cambodia. However, by 1986 this guide had stopped, a Khmer Rouge representative expressing that while the tribesmen were "extremely, daring", they had "no support from any authority" and "no political vision".

Following the suspension of supplies, the unpleasant guerrilla warfare would anyway in time decrease FULRO's powers to close to two or three hundred. In 1980 a unit of more than 200 warriors had to divide from and take shelter in Khmer Rouge on the Thai-Cambodian fringe. General Chavalit prompted them to look for displaced person status through UNHCR. When this was allowed they were moved to North Carolina in the U.S.

In August 1992 columnist Nate Thayer went to Mondulkiri and visited the last FULRO base. Thayer educated the group that FULRO's leader Y Bham Enuol had been executed by the Khmer Rouge seventeen years already. The FULRO troops gave up their weapons in October 1992; huge numbers of this group were given haven in the United States. Even at this late stage, they possibly chose to surrender furnished battle when they at long last heard that Y Bham Enuol had been executed in April 1975.

Chapter 7: Combat history

A settlement program of Kinh Vietnamese by the South Vietnamese government and joined Vietnamese Communist government was actualized. The South Vietnamese and Communist Vietnamese settlement of the Central Highlands have been contrasted with the historic Nam tiến of past Vietnamese rulers.

The Central Highlands Montagnards, Cham, and Delta Cambodians (Khmer Krom) were altogether estranged by the South Vietnamese government under Diem. The Montagnard Highlands were exposed to settlement with ethnic Vietnamese by Diem. A total dismissal of Vietnamese principle was felt by non-NLF clans of the Montagnards in 1963.

The Chinese, Khmer, and Chams were victimized by the South Vietnamese GVN, despite the fact that the GVN treated Montagnards much more terrible than the three past ethnicities, causing Montagnards to revolt again by venturing to treat a whole Montagnard town as disposable pawn. The South Vietnamese and the NLF (Viet Cong) attacked the evacuee camps occupied by Montagnards in Dalat during the Tet offensive. In the Central Highlands, Montagnard land was exposed to an endeavored seizure by the South Vietnamese Madame Nguyễn Cao Kỳ in 1971. 9 Montagnards and 3 Chinese were chosen for South Vietnam's protected get together after weight was actualized on the government.

Y'Bham brought FULRO to the fore in 1965 while hostile to South

Vietnamese propaganda was coordinated towards CIDG troops by FULRO flyers assaulting the Saigon system and hailing Cambodia for its support since Prince Norodom Sihanouk propelled the Indochinese People's gathering in March 1963 with Y'Bham to reveal insight into the Montagnard situation.

The Highlander head Y Bham, Cham pioneer Les Kosem and Cambodian pioneer Sihanouk were altogether photographed together at the gathering where they announced their war against the South Vietnamese and America for the sake of the Khmer, Cham, and highlander peoples.

Y'Bham accomplished control in 1965 and CIDG individuals were asked by FULRO to abscond while the South Vietnamese specialists were assaulted by FULRO which lauded Cambodia under Prince Norodom Sihanouk, who advanced the "Indochinese People's Conference" at Phom Penh in 1963 which was gone to by Y'Bham.

Neighboring Vietnam, the Cambodian woods were abused as a base by FULRO warriors doing combating the Democratic Republic of Vietnam.

The undermining secessionist group FULRO established during the 1960s in South Vietnam by the clans of the highland ethnic minorities.

The US Special Forces and Sihanouk supported the FULRO Montagnard contenders who were battling against the South Vietnamese.

The Montagnard occupied Central Highlands got open to the Vietnamese just under French standard. The word savage (moi) was utilized by the Vietnamese against the Montagnard Degars. Both the South Vietnamese and the assembled Communist Vietnam government were battled against by the FULRO Degar warriors for the Central Highlands and Montagnard individuals under the bearing of Y-Bham Enuol. The war lead to the passings of 200,000 Degar individuals. Degar courts were nullified by South Vietnam and the Central Highlands got overflowed with Vietnamese pilgrims under the bearing of South Vietnam. Torture and mass captures by the Vietnamese military were utilized in the CEntral Highlands against the Degar during the February 2001 fights against Vietnamese oppression.

A report on Vietnamese abuse of Montagnards was given by Human Rights Watch titled "Restraint of Montagnards: Conflicts Over Land and Religion in Vietnam's Central Highlands".

The lowlander Vietnamese seized Montagnard lands, assaulted their way of life and language, and masscred the Monyagnards because of their scorn against them and their particular religion, culture, language, and ethnicity (Malayo-Polynesian) marks them separated to the Vietnamese. They were alluded to as savage "moi" by the Vietnamese. The Vietnamese abused them for many years.

They were amazing at trailing and chasing targets. It was under French guideline when the highlands were first exposed to Vietnamese settlement. Preceding the division the previous brought together Vietnam had mishandled and abused the Montagnards so South Vietnamese and North Vietnamese the same were focused on and despised by the Montagnards during the war because of the separation and prejudice against the Montagnards at the hands of the Vietnamese.

7.1 Uprising during the Republic of Vietnam

In 1958 the Central Highlands was a scene of a revolt by the local tribals against osmosis and settlement of the land by the Vietnamese executed by the South Vietnamese government. Neither the National Liberation Front (Viet Cong) nor South Vietnamese were on FULRO which Prince Sihanouk supported after its establishing in 1964 from an association of different highlander tribals. The war prompted the passings of a gigantic measure of the ancestral locals because of the battling which went on all through the highlands.

The new changes to the economy and living in the Central Highlands incited the tribals to began FULRO to oppose the South Vietnamese with the guide of Sihanouk.

Y'Bham Enuol built up FULRO whose sole normal bond and belief system was against Vietnamese sentiment, with flawed faithfulness to whatever else, made in 1964, situated in Ratanakiri and Mondolkiri areas in Cambodia and the Central Highlands in Vietnam of the neighborhood mountaineers.

The Viet Cong and Cambodia drew nearer FULRO after its foundation.

The Cambodian Prince Sihanouk upheld the formation of FULRO which was shaped out of an assembled coalition of South Vietnam's diverse slope innate peoples.

The South Vietnamese abuse of the highlanders caused the formation of FULRO and it worked from Cambodia with support by Sihanouk so as to oppose the persecution, two commonplace capitals were seized by FULRO in December 1965 and FULRO constrained the South Vietnam to give concessions.

There was for quite some time set up enmity between the mountain tribesman and lowland Vietnamese. Montagnards battled against South Vietnamese officers in Pleiku, Darlac, and Quang Quc. The Tribal mountain people groups joined in FULRO propelled uprisings in Darlac, Lac Thin. Phu Tien went under Montagnard rule after they caused substantial misfortunes on South Vietnamese fighters, rising up in Phu Bon and engaging South Vietnamese soldiers.

Portrayal and an autonomous political element were among the correspondences expressed as their objectives by FULRO against South Vietnam.

During the uprising, hostile to government Montagnard Rhade radicals from CIDG butchered South Vietnamese soldiers and held onto American troopers as detainees, after the uprising a portion of the Montagnards joined the Montagnard nonconformist development FULRO drove by Y-Bham Enuol in Cambodia. The Montagnards got Prince Sihanouk and Cham support and were not associated with the Viet Cong.

The prompting for the uprising is had faith in certain quarters to have begun from Cambodia (Phnom Penh) where innate heads against the Vietnamese had congregated before the FULRO uprising on September 20 at Ban-Me-Thuot.

The state objective was "freedom" from mistreatment endured by minorities at the hands of South Vietnam and the Montagnards, Chams, and Khmers were altogether affirmed to be represented by FULRO.

The South Vietnamse government in Saigon sent a strategic unforeseen in August 1968 to Ban Me Thuot to haggle with FULRO agents including Y Bham Enuol after a guarantee of safe lead was given to him by Tran Van Huong, the Prime Minister of South Vietnam, after FULRO individuals at Camp Le Rolland consented to haggle since South Vietnam was never again the top need for Cambodia in light of the fact that the Khmer Rouge was beginning to divert Sihanouk in 1968.

Montagnard ladies were manhandled (tortured) at the hands of Vietcong forces.

The Cambodian Cham Les Kosem, a Lieutenant Colonel, was answerable for issues identifying with ethnic minorities under Sihanouk and both Kosem and Sihanouk knew about FULRO.

The three stripes on the banner of FULRO spoke to the unification of the "Battle Front of the Khmer of Lower Cambodia", the "Front for the Liberation of Champa", and "Bajarka Movement" after Y-Dhon Adrong was persuaded to combine them by Cham pioneer Les Kosem during the Montagnard uprising against South Vietnam.

While in Cambodia at FULRO base camp, Y-Bham had his family moved into Mondul Kiri's Krechea by means of Vietnam's Darlac and Ban Don zones.

The South Vietnamese Truong Son was commanded by Barry Peterson and Peterson was irate when Y-Preh, a FULRO part needed to meet him since contact was precluded with the agitators who were battling against South Vietnam.

After the Montagnard uprising against South Vietnam, 10 months went before FULRO consented to haggle with South Vietnam.

After Colonel Freund consented to yield and surrender a base to the South Vietnamese, the Montagnards in the Buon Sarpa unit were incredibly disappointed and discontent.

The 1950s BAJARKA development preceded FULRO which was its successor.

While the Bajaraka development established, it is accepted that parallel to it the foundation of the "Front for the Liberation of Champa" took place.

FULRO reports contained the marks of and FULRO gatherings were gone to by individuals from Front for the Liberation of Champa. A Cham goddess' name was utilized as a call sign by Les Kosem.

The FULRO associations was supported by Prince Sihanouk of Cambodia, hostile to Vietnamese and against American Frenchmen, and it was endeavored to be utilized against the Vietcong's NFL by the Americans because of their ill will towards Vietnamese.

The Front de libération du Kampuchea Nord, the Front de libération du Kampuchea Krom, the Front de libération du Champa shaped FULRO in 1964 after the Khmer Krom, the PMS minorities (Montagnards), and both Vietnam Cham and Cambodian participated in solidarity together to battle the Vietnamese.

In 1963 the "Mouvement Khmer-Serei" was begun against the Saigon government by Norodom Sihanouk's legislature.

The Malayo-Polynésian and Mon-Khmer ethnic minorities who were against the South Vietnamese Saigon government consolidated in September 1964, for example, the Cambodian government support "Front de Libération du Champa".

The rebel developments were urged to look for autonomy as the Khmer government supported FULRO at the Indochinese People's conference.

The Front de Libération du Champa banner incorporated a Crescent star.

Lon Nol upheld FULRO slope clans, and in South Vietnam and Cambodia's boondocks area he battled an intermediary war against the NLF by means of Khmer Krom separations as he wanted to copy Van Pao.

The settlement of ethnic Vietnamese from thickly populated territories to mitigate the money related weight on those zones on the lands of the tribals in the Central Highlands was supported by the Vietnamese government and it prompted the formation of FULRO to oppose the Vietnamese.

A "freed zone" filled in as the base for the head of FULRO, making their objectives misty, being an association established by Montagnards, Cham, and Khmer Krom and mounted an uprising against South Vietnam as they worked in Cambodia close Darlac in the Central Highlands.

Kuno Knöbl attempted to examine FULRO with the Pleiku-based Special Forces Captain Schwikar who would not discuss it.

FULRO helped toppled the South Vietnamese government. The Vietnamese Communists utilized planes to bomb FULRO warriors as they rebelled against the "re-instruction", monetary arrangements and different approaches which influenced their lifestyle which were actualized by the Vietnamese Communists. With Cambodian support, Montagnard FULRO warriors battled against the Vietnamese Communist administration of bound together Vietnam until 1992.

7.2 Vietnamese settlement

A settlement program of Kinh Vietnamese by the South Vietnamese government and joined Vietnamese Communist government was executed. Forgetting about any designs for autonomy for ethnic minorities, a digestion plan was propelled by the South Vietnamese government with the making of the "Social and Economic Council for the Southern Highlander Country", the South Vietnamese based their way to deal with the highlanders by asserting that they would be "created" since they were "poor" and "uninformed", making swidden agriculturalists sedentarize and settling ethnic Vietnamese from the seaside districts into the highlands, for example, Northern Vietnamese Catholic outcasts who fled to South Vietnam, 50,000 Vietnamese pilgrims were in the highlands in 1960 and in 1963 the total number of pioneers was 200,000 and up to 1974 the South Vietnamese were as yet executed the settlement plan despite the fact that the highland locals experienced monstrous disturbance and confusion in view of the settlement,

The South Vietnamese government made just representative, futile concessions to ethnic minorities so as to stop FULRo from picking up support.

FULRO tribals ascended in an uprising against Diem's settlement of the Highlands with ethnic Vietnamese settlers.

In 1955 the Central Highlands were overwhelmed with Northern Vietnamese transients after the autonomous Montagnard zone was abrogated by Ngô Đình Diệm. Y Bham Enoul established Bajaraka on January 5, 1958 to oppose the segregation, Vietnamese settlement on Highlands and constrained osmosis by the South Vietnamese government. The United Nations Secretary General and outside government offices were reached by Y Bham Enuol. He was slaughtered by the Khmer Rouge on April 20, 1975.

An uprising against South Vietnam was propelled by Bajaraka head Y Bham Enoul with Montagnard Monong and Rhade fighters who held onto American Special Forces and some Vietnamese as detainees in their CIDG bases in the wake of holding onto a Ban Me Thuot based radio broadcast and incurring 70 passings upon the Vietnamese when taking over Darlac CIDG puts together with 3,000 soldiers with respect to September 19, 1964. Ruler Sihanouk's organization in Cambodia guided FULRO with against SEATO, hostile to American belief system and in 1965 FULRO discharged maps indicating that their definitive objective was for Montagnard and Cham freedom inside a resuscitated new Champa state and for Khmers to retake Cochinchina, confirming the announcement Notre yet est de défendre notre survie et notre patrimoine culturel, spirituel et racial, et ainsi l'Indépendence de nos Pays. which was found in their presentation which likewise asserted that ethnic minorities were being exposed to massacre at th hands of the South Vietnamese, requiring the Montagnards, Khmer Krom and Cham to solidarity in FULRO under the course of their Haut Comité on September 20, 1964. CIDG bases were the place the majority were found while it was in Cambodia where the head of FULRO were based and from where the FULRO Montagnard, Cham, and Khmer Krom boss coordinated the uprising.

The push to free the Cham individuals was driven by Major General Les Kosem. The Cham individuals keep the spirit of FULRO alive as indicated by previous FULRO Cham part Po Dharma who went a voyage to see Les Kosem's grave.

Quang Van Du was the lawful enrolled name of the Cham Po Dharma. He stood against ethnic Kinh Vietnamese domineering jerks for his individual Cham while he was in school and helped spread Cham patriot thoughts against the South Vietnamese. He turned into an individual from FULRO and went to a FULRO preparing camp in Cambodia and battled in Mondulkiri. While in Cambodia he assaulted the North Vietnamese and South Vietnamese consulates and then he battled against Vietnamese Communists. Subsequent to being injured in fight he quit his military profession in the wake of looking for the consent of Les Kosem himself and went to France to be instructed and serve FULRO in a non military personnel capacity.

A settlement program of indigenous individuals' land in the Central Highlands with Vietnamese officers and pioneers was actualized by South Vietnamese pioneer Ngo Dinh Diem beginning in 1955. The Highlander Liberation Front was established in 1955 during a gathering of indigenous highlands who had initially mobilized to the Rade Y Thih Eban against the South Vietnamese government. In 1960 in Phnom Penh the establishment of the Les Kosem drove "Champa Liberation Front" and "Kampuchia Krom Liberation Front" happened to battle against South Vietnamese settlement.

FULRO attempted to make a sovereign and self-overseeing Central

Highlands through uprising against the South Vietnamese for 10 years while situated in Cambodia's Mondulkiri territory with support from Prime Minister Lon Nol of Cambodia, drove by Cham Lieutenant Major Les Kosem and Rhade pioneer Y Bham Enuol yet when the Khmer Rouge came to control, they assaulted FULRO. Les Kosem fled the nation while the French international safe haven shielded other fULRO pioneers, anyway political resistance was abused when the FULRO pioneers were seized and executed by the Khmer Rouge in the wake of storming the consulate. The North Vietnamese and Khmer Rouge adequately finished FULRO anyway components of FULRO still endure and chose to take up arms against the new Communist Vietnamese administration of brought together Vietnam as they had against the South Vietnamese. FULRO got support from China and Cambodian components against Vietnam. The Vietnamese attack of Cambodia was battled against by Dega FULRO remnants.

7.3 During the Socialist Republic of Vietnam

All types of Vietnamese mastery were restricted by FULRO tribesman in the Central Highlands and they proceeded with the battle against the assembled Vietnamese Communist government after the fall of South Vietnam.

In the novel For the Sake of All Living Things it was noticed that both enemy of Communist and Communist, Vietnamese all in all were battled against by the FULRO mountain dwellers in the highlands.

Y Bham Enuol, the head of FULRO alongside 150 different individuals stowed away in the French consulate when the Khmer Rouge took over Phnom Penh, anyway the Khmer Rouge constrained the French representative to give up them all to their custody and had them killed.

The counter South Vietnam, and hostile to Communist Vietnam FULRO which battled both the South Vietnamese and the Communist Vietnamese, was given guide and help by China by means of Thailand to battle against the Vietnamese all through the 1970s and 1980s while China likewise supported ethnic minorities in northern Vietnam along the outskirt against the Vietnamese.

China sponsored the Central Highlands-based FULRO Koho, Rhade, Jarai, and Bahnar warriors to fight the Vietnamese PAVN in the areas of Dac Lac,

Kontum, and Gai Lai where Vietnamese military and police headquarters were ambushed by the fighters.

China, North Vietnam ethnic minorities, the FULRO Montagnards, conservative Laotians, Prince Sihanouk, conservative Cambodians under Son Sann, and the Thai were all enemy of Communist groups reached by Truong Nhu Tang who was an individual from the Committee for National Salvation which was against the Communist Vietnamese government.

The FULRO Montagnard warriors got military materials from China in 1980.

Hostile to Vietnamese Laotian associations and FULRO alongside Cambodian (Khmer) associations were upheld by China.

The way of life of the Montagnards was focused for eradication by the Vietnamese and there were a very long time of warfare between the Vietnamese and Montagnards. Attack rifles, carbines, rockets, explosives, and ammo were among the weapons the remaining Montagnard FULRO warriors previously possessed when they surrendered the battle and gave them to the United Nations in 1992.

FULRO contenders in the wildernesses of Mondulkiri who were battling against the Vietnamese were met in 1992 by Nate Thayer.

7.4 Other minority obstruction groups

The Montagnards in FULRO battled the Vietnamese for a long time after the finish of the Vietnam War and the size of Vietnamese assaults on the Montagnards came to destructive extents with the butcher of more than 200,000 Montagnards after 1975. The Vietnamese butchered 200,000 Montagnards after 1975 during the war among FULRO and Vietnam in the Central Highlands, as the Vietnamese rent land for Japanese organizations to collect wood in the zone. Weapons, weapons, and 5,000 rifles were given by the Chinese to the Montagnards after the Montagnards mentioned help from China by means of Thai General Savit-Yun K-Yut since the United States would not help the FULRO Montagnards against the Vietnamese.

FULRO was upheld by China. The wild revolt against the Vietnamese Communist legislature of bound together Vietnam by FULRO included 12,000 warriors in the Central Highlands. Vietnamese government laborers were assaulted in their offices and houses by guerilla separations of FULRO warriors starting from Cambodia and mountain regions.

The Central Highlands had a mystery course by means of Cambodia to China where FULRO warriors were given Chinese guide and help through weapons and money. In the regions of Dac Lac, Kontum, and Gai Lai, Vietnamese armies of troopers and police were attacked by the Koho, Rhade, Jarai, and Bahnar FULRO fighters.

Hostile to North-Vietnam Laotian Hmong revolutionaries and the counter South Vietnamese FULRO both got support from China and Thailand to battle against the Communist legislature of bound together Vietnam.

There was high versatility among ethnic minorities like the Hmong, Yao, Nung, and Tai over the outskirt among China and Vietnam.

At the Laotian fringe Hmong radicals sponsored by China battled. After the United States stopped helping the Hmong, the Chinese help was looked for by the Hmong fighters.

In Phong Saly territory of Laos, Meo (Hmong) contenders were supported by the Chinese against the Laotian government which was a partner of Vietnam.

Zao, Lu, and Khmu ethnic minorities were additionally sponsored in Phou Bia against the Vietnamese by China.

The Vietnamese executed any individuals from its ethnic minorities along the outskirt with China who worked for the Chinese.

Help and help originated from China by means of Kunming in Yunnan to hostile to Vietnamese associations in Laos, Cambodia (Kampuchea) and FULRO in Vietnam to frame an assembled alliance against Vietnam.

In the upper east region of Cambodia assaults were led by joined FULRO powers and Cambodian guerillas battling against Vietnam from Preah Vihear.

Laos and Cambodia (Kampuchea) based enemy of Vietnamese associations were courses of support from China to a FULRO like group which was established and made out of "slope people groups" from Laos and Cambodia.

Laotian and Cambodian associations battling against the Vietnamese were a travel point by means of which Chinese support came to FULRO like organizations.

7.5 Post-Insurgency

A 2002 article in the Washington Times revealed that Montagnard ladies were exposed to constrained mass disinfection by the Vietnamese government for the Montagnard's populace to be decreased, notwithstanding taking lands of the Montagnards, and assaulting their strict convictions, killing and tortuting them in a type of "crawling genocide",

Luke Simpkins, a MP in the House of Representatives of Australia censured the Vietnamese mistreatment of the Central Highland Montagnards and noticing both the South Vietnamese government and system of bound together Communist Vietnam assaulted the Montagnards and vanquished their lands, referencing FULRO which battled against the Vietnamese and the longing for the Montagnards to save their way of life and language. The Vietnamse government has non-Montagnards choose Montagnard land and murdered Montagnards in the wake of imprisoning them. There were 200,000 Montagnard passings to the war.

Previous Green Beret and author Don Bendell composed a novel dependent on Vietnam's strategies in the Central Highlands with subtleties in his book, for example, blaming the Communist Vietnamese government actualized a destructive and discriminatory arrangement against the local Montagnards in the Central Highlands, prohibiting Montagnard dialects and executing Vietnamese language, having Vietnamese men wed Montagnard young ladies and ladies by power, colonizing the Central Highlands with huge measures of Vietnamese pioneers structure the lowlands, delivering fear and on the Montagnards with the Cong An, and causing them to perform slave work, raising estates for elastic, tea, and coffee on the Central Highlands in the wake of wrecking the vegetation in the region and due to these "politically-sanctioned racial segregation like conditions".

7.6 Khmer Krom

Cambodia used to in the past claim Kampuchea Krom whose indigenous occupants were ethnic Cambodian Khmers before the settling Vietnamese entered by means of Champa. The element of Vietnam under pioneer French principle got the Khmer lands of Kampuchea Krom from France on 4 June 1949. Vietnam mistreats the Khmer Krom and the separatists among the Khmer Krom think about Vietnamese control as pilgrim rule. The Vietnamese gave new Vietnamese names to the Kampuchea Krom areas they bit by bit seized.

Seizure of land and abuse of Khmer Krom Buddhist Monks by the Vietnamese were issues raised during a goals against Vietnam passed by the European Parliament by Khmer Krom protestors.

Khmer Krom still sharply review the day that the Vietnamese got the 21 regions of Kampuchea Krom from the French on 4 June 1949. The Cambodian Kampuchea Krom were the locals of the district and were not counseled on the choice made to give the land to the Vietnamese by the French. The Vietnamese suppressed the Khmer content and Khmer language, assaulting the way of life, religion and books of the Khmer Krom. Individuals who showed against land seizures by the Vietnamese were imprisoned by the Vietnamese Communists. Khmer patriotism is a solid obstacle to the pulverization of Khmer Krom character by the Vietnamese. The Vietnamese have imprisoned and murdered Khmer Krom during the 64 years of rule after the French transfer.

Chau Dara, a Buddhist priest, established the Khmer Krom development "Battle Front of the Khmer of Kampuchea Krom" because of strategies of the South Vietnamese government like having Khmer Krom land in the Mekong Delta vanquished by Vietnamese Kinh, hostile to Buddhist arrangement and constrained osmosis into Vietnamese culture. FULRo was made by the unification of Montagnard Bajaraka with the "Battle Front of the Khmer of Kampuchea Krom" and "Front for the Liberation of Champa" in 1964. Against Khmer Krom approaches are actualized by the Vietnamese government in view of Khmer Krom separatism.

Chapter 8 : Allegations of United States support for the Khmer Rouge

There are claims that the United States (U.S.) straightforwardly outfitted the Khmer Rouge during the Cambodian–Vietnamese War so as to debilitate the impact of Vietnam and the Soviet Union in Southeast Asia. It isn't questioned that the United States energized the administration of China to give military preparing and support to the Khmer Rouge and that the United States decided in favor of the Khmer Rouge to remain the official delegate of the nation in the United Nations considerably after 1979 when the Khmer Rouge was for the most part removed by Vietnam and managed only a little piece of the country.

Extra claimed U.S. actions that profited the Khmer Rouge extend from tolerating Chinese and Thai guide to the association (Henry Kissinger) to, as per Michael Haas, straightforwardly furnishing the Khmer Rouge. The U.S. government officially denies these cases, and Nate Thayer protected U.S. arrangement, contending that little, assuming any, American guide really arrived at the Khmer Rouge. Notwithstanding, it isn't questioned that the U.S. decided in favor of the Khmer Rouge, and later, for the Coalition Government of Democratic Kampuchea (CGDK), which was overwhelmed by the Khmer Rouge, to hold Cambodia's United Nations (UN) seat until 1982 and 1991, respectively.

Be that as it may, as Secretary of State Edmund Muskie stated, these actions were a result of Vietnam's refusal to pull back troops, so there was never support for the Khmer Rouge:

Not the slightest bit infers any support or acknowledgment of the Democratic Kampuchea system. We detest and denounce the system's human rights record and could never support its arrival to control in Phnom Penh.

The Khmer Rouge, the socialist party drove by Pol Pot that managed Cambodia after its 1975 victory in the Cambodian Civil War, executed the Cambodian decimation, which somewhere in the range of 1975 and 1979 murdered somewhere in the range of 1.5 and 2 million individuals, almost 25% of Cambodia's population. During the destruction, China was the fundamental worldwide supporter of the Khmer Rouge, supplying "in excess of 15,000 military guides" and the vast majority of its outside aid.

8.1 Vietnamese invasion

Vietnam attacked Cambodia in late 1978 and built up the People's Republic of Kampuchea (PRK) drove by Khmer Rouge defectors. Vietnam's intrusion was inspired by rehashed cross-outskirt assaults by the Khmer Rouge that focused Vietnamese regular citizens, including the Ba Chúc slaughter—in which the Khmer Rouge methodicallly murdered the whole populace of a Vietnamese town of more than 3,000 individuals, except for one lady who endure being shot in the neck and clubbed, making her languish difficult migraines over an amazing remainder; before being executed, a large number of the unfortunate casualties were "primitively tortured." These assaults executed more than 30,000 Vietnamese in total.

Vietnam expelled the Khmer Rouge and finished the massacre in an insignificant 17 days, nonetheless, Vietnamese soldiers occupied Cambodia for the following eleven years. Following the intrusion, Vietnam endeavored to promote the wrongdoings of the Khmer Rouge, building up an ossuary for the unfortunate casualties at Ba Chúc and persuading the PRK to do likewise for the Khmer Rouge's Cambodian exploited people; the Khmer Rouge's most notorious jail, S-21—which held 20,000 detainees, "everything except seven" of whom were killed—was uncovered in May 1979 and in the end transformed into the Tuol Sleng Genocide Museum, despite the fact that there were well more than 150 Khmer Rouge concentration camps "on a similar model, at any rate one for each district."

To rebuff Vietnam for toppling the Khmer Rouge, China attacked Vietnam in February 1979, while the United States (U.S.) "simply slapped more endorses on Vietnam" and "blocked credits from the International Monetary Fund (IMF) to Vietnam."

China prepared Khmer Rouge fighters on its dirt during 1979—1986 (if not later), "positioned military counselors with Khmer Rouge troops as late as 1990," and "supplied in any event $1 billion in military guide" during the 1980s. After the 1991 Paris Peace Accords, Thailand kept on permitting the Khmer Rouge "to exchange and move over the Thai outskirt to continue their exercises ... albeit worldwide analysis, especially from the U.S. and Australia ... made it deny passing any immediate military support."

8.2 Cambodia's UN seat

Because of Chinese and Western resistance to the Vietnamese attack and occupation, the Khmer Rouge, as opposed to the PRK, was permitted to hold Cambodia's United Nations (UN) seat until 1982. After 1982, the UN seat was filled by a Khmer Rouge-commanded alliance—the Coalition Government of Democratic Kampuchea (CGDK).

Undisputed US support

The U.S. allowed Thailand to permit the Khmer Rouge to utilize bases in Thailand to wage a war of revolt against the legislature in Phnom Penh that had been introduced by Vietnam. Elizabeth Becker detailed that U.S. National Security Advisor Zbigniew Brzezinski asserted that he "created convincing Thailand to coordinate completely with China to in endeavors to rebuild the Khmer Rouge."

The U.S. given a great many dollars of yearly nourishment help to 20,000-

40,000 Khmer Rouge guerillas in Khmer Rouge bases in Thailand. The guide was overseen by an association that the U.S. built up in the U.S. government office in Bangkok called the Kampuchean Emergency Group (KEG) staffed by U.S. Focal Intelligence Agency faculty and headed by Michael Eiland, whose activity involved deciphering satellite reconnaissance photos of Cambodia, and who had been tasks officer of a U.S. commando surveillance unit code-named "Daniel Boone" and later was named U.S. Barrier Intelligence Agency boss accountable for the Southeast Asia Region.

US National Security Advisor, Zbigniew Brzezinski recognized that "I encouraged the Chinese to support Khmer Rouge leader Pol Pot ... we would never support him, yet China could." However, Brzezinski accordingly expressed: "The Chinese were supporting Pol Pot, yet with no assistance or game plan from the United States. In addition, we told the Chinese expressly that in our view Pol Pot was an evil entity and that the United States would have nothing to do with him—legitimately or indirectly."

Beam Cline, a previous representative director of the U.S. Focal Intelligence Agency visited a Khmer Rouge camp inside Cambodia in November 1980 as a delegate of the approaching organization of U.S President Ronald Reagan. The Thai Foreign Ministry denied that Cline had unlawfully crossed into Cambodia, however secretly recognized that Cline had visited the Pol Pot camp. Khmer Rouge strategic agents to the United Nations had openly reported the Cline excursion to the Pol Pot camp in Cambodia.

In late 1975, previous National Security Advisor and United States Secretary of State Henry Kissinger told the Thai outside priest: "You should tell the Cambodians that we will be companions with them. They are lethal hooligans however we won't let that stand in our way." Years after the fact, Kissinger explained: "The Thais and the Chinese didn't need a Vietnamese-commanded Indochina. We didn't need the Vietnamese to rule. I don't accept we did anything for Pol Pot. Be that as it may, I speculate we shut our eyes when some others accomplished something for Pol Pot."

Cambodian pioneer Norodom Sihanouk, when gotten some information about charges of advantage in May 1987 . likewise supports the Khmer Rouge. Indeed, even before the framing of the Coalition Government in 1982, the U.S. every year casted a ballot for the Khmer Rouge system. ... The U.S.A. says that it is against the Khmer Rouge, that it is master Sihanouk, ace Son

Sann. Be that as it may, the demons, they are there laughs with Sihanouk and Son Sann."

8.3 Allegations of U.S. military support

U.S. support for the Khmer Rouge guerrillas during the 1980s was "critical" to keeping the association alive, and was to a limited extent roused by vengeance over Vietnam's destruction of the U.S. during the Vietnam War, as per Tom Fawthrop. A WikiLeaks dump of 500,000 U.S. strategic links from 1978 archive shows that the organization of President Jimmy Carter was torn between repugnance at the monstrosities of the Khmer Rouge and worry with the probability of developing Vietnamese impact should the Khmer Rouge collapse.

Sovereign Norodom Sihanouk, pioneer of an opposition group aligned with the Khmer Rouge in the war against the Phnom Penh government, recognized that CIA guides were available in Khmer Rouge camps in late 1989.

As per Michael Haas, regardless of openly denouncing the Khmer Rouge, the U.S. offered military support to the association and was instrumental in counteracting UN acknowledgment of the Vietnam-adjusted government. Haas contended that the U.S. and China reacted to endeavors from the Association of South East Asian Nations (ASEAN) for incapacitating the Khmer Rouge by guaranteeing the Khmer Rouge remained furnished, and that U.S. endeavors for consolidating the Khmer Rouge with united factions brought about the arrangement of the CGDK. After 1982, the U.S. expanded its yearly secret guide to the Cambodian opposition from $4 million to $10 million.

On the other hand, Nate Thayer described that "The United States has scrupulously kept away from any immediate contribution in helping the Khmer Rouge", rather giving non-deadly guide to non-socialist Khmer People's National Liberation Front (KPNLF) and Armee Nationale Sihanouk (ANS) extremists, which once in a while helped out the Khmer Rouge on the combat zone, regardless of being alliance accomplices, and which battled with the Khmer Rouge many occasions preceding 1987. As per Thayer, "In months spent in regions constrained by the three opposition groups and during scores of experiences with the Khmer Rouge ... I not even once experienced guide given to the non-socialist resistance being used by or possessing the Khmer Rouge."

8.4 Leakage of US arms to Khmer Rouge

Joel Brinkley expressed that, in spite of the fact that U.S. arrangement was to offer help to "15,000 insufficient 'noncommunist' rebel warriors", "charges made the rounds that a portion of the American guide, $215 million up until now, was discovering its way to the Khmer Rouge." A resulting examination drove by Thomas Fingar of the United States Department of State's Bureau of Intelligence and Research (INR) "discovered some spillage—including sharing of ammo, joint barrier of an extension, and utilizing one truck to move both 'noncommunist' and Khmer Rouge contenders to a battle." Fingar was contemptuous of his own investigators' report, which he portrayed as an "epiphenomenon in an insect bazaar": "Isn't the bigger target here crushing the Vietnamese puppets in Phnom Penh?"

Chapter 9 : Nong Chan Refugee Camp

Nong Chan Refugee Camp, situated in Nong Chan Village, Khok Sung District, Sa Kaeo Province, Thailand, was one of the most punctual composed displaced person camps on the Thai-Cambodian outskirt, where thousands of Khmer evacuees looked for nourishment and social insurance subsequent to escaping the Vietnamese attack of Democratic Kampuchea in 1979. It was decimated by the Vietnamese military in late 1984, after which its populace was moved to Site Two Refugee Camp.

A Khmer Serei camp was set up close to the Thai town of Ban Nong Chan at some point during the 1950s by Cambodians contradicted to the standard of Prince Norodom Sihanouk. It was populated predominantly by bandits and bootleggers until the mid-1970s, when evacuees escaping from the Khmer Rouge framed an opposition development there. On June 8, 1979 the Thai military moved a few thousand outcasts from Nong Chan to the outskirt close to the sanctuary of Prasat Preah Vihear where the exiles were coercively repatriated into a minefield on the Cambodian side of the border.

In late August 1979 Kong Sileah, a previous maritime officer, built up the MOULINAKA obstruction power at Nong Chan. Kong Sileah demanded that his around 100 guerrillas remain separate from the 13,000 regular people in the camp; he got known for honesty in his dealings with help agencies. Encouraged by the great request of the camp, the International Committee of the Red Cross (ICRC) constructed an emergency clinic there.

On November 8, 1979 a battle broke out in the camp when a Thai officer was blamed for assaulting a Khmer lady and was shot to death. The Thai military commander Colonel Prachak Sawaengchit requested his soldiers to shell Nong Chan (referred to around then as Camp 51), slaughtering around 100 displaced people. The occurrence got universal consideration in light of the fact that U.S. First Lady Rosalynn Carter was booked to visit Sa Kaeo Refugee Camp on the accompanying day.

9.1 Robert Ashe's "Land Bridge"

In November 1979 Kong Sileah met with Robert Patrick Ashe, a five-year veteran of helpful work in Thailand and recommended that nourishment ought to be dispersed at Nong Chan for Cambodians to bring home to the interior. This started the well known "land connect", a genuinely fruitful endeavor to convey nourishment, ranch tools and seeds to Khmers living inside Kampuchea. Starting on December 12, Ashe and Kong Sileah sorted out deliberate appropriations utilizing camp administrators to give somewhere in the range of 10 and 30 kilograms of rice to individuals landing from inside Cambodia. These voyagers landed by walking, by bike, and in oxcarts. By Christmas 1979 twelve truckloads of rice were being appropriated day by day to more than 6,000 people.

Van Saren, a warlord in the neighboring camp of Mak Mun who had made a fortune selling rice that had been circulated by help organizations, chose that Nong Chan spoke to a danger to his influence, as the cost of rice fell significantly once the land connect started working. He assaulted Nong Chan on December 30, purportedly with the guide of the Royal Thai Army and torched the medical clinic. Nourishment conveyance continued a couple of days after Van Saren's assault, and by mid-January 10,000 individuals daily were getting rice. Kong Sileah left the camp and moved with his troopers into the inside of occupied Kampuchea, living in natural conditions in the woodland, a factor which may have added to his demise from cerebral jungle fever on August 16, 1980. After this, Nong Chan went under the control of Chea Chhut, a warlord with less scruples than Kong Sileah.

9.2 Seed distribution

Numerous expectations of a broad starvation in Kampuchea prodded UNICEF, the Food and Agriculture Organization, ICRC, the World Food Program, and a few nongovernmental help offices to support the seed-conveyance program. After a preliminary dissemination of 220 tons of rice seeds at Nong Chan on March 21, World Relief and CARE each dispersed 2000 tons of rice seed to more than 68,000 ranchers in early April. Many ranchers who got seed at Nong Chan whined that they didn't have the tools with which to plant the rice. World Relief, Christian Outreach and Oxfam reacted in May by disseminating cultivator heads, furrow tips, rope, fishnets, and fishhooks, just as oxcarts. During that month 340,000 individuals got nourishment and seeds at Nong Chan.

UNICEF and the ICRC were at first contradicted to an enormous seed circulation program since they expected that it would pull in ranchers forever into the camps, having made the adventure to the fringe, despite the fact that others contended that It was the best way to give ranchers a motivating force to stay on the land. The ICRC was additionally especially wary about running a huge scale activity without first surveying the disposition of the Heng Samrin government. ICRC consequently endeavored to limit accumulating and to keep the size of the program little by forcing roofs on both the total amounts of seed that could be disseminated and on levels of appropriation in any one day. UNICEF and WFP from the start shared ICRC's alert yet turned out to be progressively loose after it turned out to be certain that the Heng Samrin government had no solid issues with the program. Although the Vietnam-sponsored government in Phnom Penh would not permit CARE and ICRC to disperse seed rice inside Kampuchea, officials didn't keep Khmer townspeople from venturing out to Nong Chan to get rice, and in a couple of cases really empowered it.

9.3 What the Land Bridge achieved

The seed dispersion at the land connect at long last finished on June 20, having given out exactly 25,521 tons of seed, alongside tools and even compost. The 1980 gather in Kampuchea, albeit not exactly 50% of prewar levels, far surpassed expectations. Approximately 50,000 tons of nourishment rice were likewise handed out to more than 700,000 Cambodians before the nourishment circulation program finished on January 23, 1981. Although pundits charge that quite a bit of this rice was exchanged or used to supply troops in both Thailand and Cambodia, the land connect was viewed as a triumph, basically on the grounds that it urged Cambodians to stay on their homesteads as opposed to moving to the exile camps in Thailand. In mid-1980, Robert Patrick Ashe was awarded the MBE (Member of the Most Excellent Order of the British Empire) for his work among evacuees.

9.4 1980 Vietnamese incursion

On June 23, 1980 around 200 Vietnamese troopers assaulted Mak Mun and Nong Chan, constraining many evacuees again into Kampuchea and executing hundreds more who resisted. Khmer fighters at Nong Chan set up a fiery safeguard, however somewhere in the range of 400 exiles were murdered and another 458 were treated at Khao-I-Dang medical clinic. Nong Chan was later recovered by Thai powers after the Vietnamese pulled back on June 24. Many displaced people moved to the close by Nong Samet Refugee Camp. were caught by the Vietnamese and walked around 25 kilometers inside Kampuchea through torrential downpour and with no safe house at night. Ashe later noted, "It was the first occasion I'd had in quite a while." Arriving in the Cambodian town of Nimitt he was questioned by a Vietnamese officer about whether nourishment help was going to anticommunist guerrillas, and following four days they were liberated and permitted to stroll over the scaffold at the fringe once again into Thailand .

9.5 Nong Chan as a base for the KPNLAF

Towards the finish of 1980 Chea Chhut was convinced by General Dien Del to unite with the Khmer People's National Liberation Front (KPNLF) and toward the finish of 1982 Nong Chan turned into the Khmer People's National Liberation Armed Forces' (KPNLAF) military central station, in spite of the fact that Ampil Camp remained the managerial home office until it was crushed in mid 1985. Nong Chan housed the KPNLAF's third, seventh and ninth contingents and an "Extraordinary Forces" unit commanded by Khmer Captain Pahn Tai that was being prepared by the British SAS with arms and help from the Malaysian Army for harm activities inside Cambodia.

As a result of its vital significance to the KPNLAF, 4000 Vietnamese soldiers supported by mounted guns and T-54 tanks assaulted Nong Chan again and wrecked it on January 31, 1983. Ground battling was accounted for outside the camp between Vietnamese soldiers situated in Cambodia and around 2000 KPNLF guerrillas. simultaneously the Vietnamese kept up a relentless blast of shells, Meanwhile, MOULINAKA units were dismissed, and KPNLF powers pulled back following a 36-hour battle. The Khao-I-Dang ICRC emergency clinic got more than 100 non military personnel wounded. Soon, notwithstanding, the camp was reoccupied and revamped.

9.6 Destruction of the camp

Somewhere in the range of 1980 and 1984 the camp was a regular objective of Vietnamese assaults. It was at long last ambushed by more than 2000 Vietnamese soldiers from the People's Army of Vietnam's (PAVN) ninth Division on November 18, 198 and authoritatively abandoned as of November 30 . The camp's populace of 30,000 outcasts was emptied to Site 3 (Ang Sila), a laterite quarry around four kilometers to the west. Another camp was built up at Site 6 (Prey Chan). Huge numbers of these exiles wound up in

Khao-I-Dang Holding Center, and the rest of resettled at Site Two Refugee
Camp in mid-1985.

Chapter 10 : Nong Samet Refugee Camp

Nong Samet Refugee Camp, situated in Nong Samet Village, Khok Sung
District, Sa Kaeo Province, Thailand, was one of the biggest displaced person
camps on the Thai-Cambodian outskirt and filled in as a power base for the
Khmer People's National Liberation Front (KPNLF) until its devastation by
the Vietnamese military in late 1984.

Displaced people started entering Thailand in enormous numbers after
Vietnam attacked Kampuchea in December 1978 and constrained the Khmer
Rouge out of power. An evacuee settlement was built up close to the Thai
town of Ban Nong Samet at some point in May 1979, and got its first
shipment of nourishment help on October 11.

The camp was initially alluded to as Chumrum Thmei (New Camp) to
recognize it from its neighbor and opponent Mak Mun Camp, which was
otherwise called Chumrum Chas (Old Camp). Nong Samet was later renamed
007 "in light of its numerous intrigues" and in August 1980 was dedicated
Rithysen, after a Khmer society legend "who endure when his siblings and
sisters were eaten up through the maneuvers of a barbarian ogress, and who
at that point deceived the ogress' daughter."

10.1 Domination by Cambodian warlords

Nong Samet Refugee Camp was found initially simply inside the Thai outskirt, around one kilometer upper east of Mak Mun and two kilometers upper east of Nong Chan. Very quickly each of the three camps were commanded via autonomous warlords who, with a few hundred unrestrained and seriously prepared guerrillas, controlled business exercises and oversaw nourishment circulation to the regular citizen population.

The camp's first head was Long Rithia, a previous infantry commander in the Khmer National Armed Forces (FANK) seventh Division who revitalized a few hundred troopers from that unit and on October 5 built up the Angkor National Liberation Movement (additionally alluded to as Khmer Angkor).

In December 1979, In-Sakhan, another previous officer from FANK who had been living on the fringe since 1975, pronounced himself pioneer of Nong Samet. He immediately understood that the size of the camp's non military personnel populace would decide his capacity base, and supported a flourishing fringe commercial center from which dealers brought appeal wares into denied Kampuchea. Within a brief timeframe Nong Samet's market pulled in thousands of merchants and dark marketeers, and the aides and gatekeepers expected to move products and money in this almost uncivilized area. Gold and valuable stones often fill in for cash on the outskirt, and In-Sakhan's fighters every now and again filled in as security accompanies.

In-Sakhan at first answered to International Committee of the Red Cross (ICRC) that the camp's populace was in any event 200,000 and help offices gave nourishment and water to 180,000 individuals until December 1979 when help laborers heard that a significant part of the nourishment was being accumulated by the warlord. At this time the circumstance on the fringe was still too confused to do a legitimate enumeration or to challenge In-Sakhan.

10.2 Rivalry with neighboring camps

Competition with neighboring camps Nong Chan and Mak Mun prompted visit outfitted savagery. In-Sakhan additionally needed to safeguard the camp against the Khmer Rouge, who propelled an assault on January 4, 1980 from close by Phnom Chat. The camp was emptied however the displaced people immediately returned.

In late January 1980, ICRC and UNICEF endeavored to sidestep In-Sakhan and disperse nourishment legitimately to Nong Samet's populace (which they presently assessed at approximately 60,000), anyway without the warlord's collaboration this demonstrated about impossible. furthermore, it gave the idea that numerous Nong Samet inhabitants had to go to Nong Chan to get nourishment in light of the fact that their apportions were being seized by In-Sakhan's soldiers.

Appropriately, in late February 1980 guide offices stopped circulating nourishment in Nong Samet altogether. After two weeks, UNICEF led a sustenance study and found across the board levels of ailing health, hindering and hunger in the camp population. ICRC chose to attempt direct conveyance to bolted warehouses inside the camp, and to permit area pioneers to circulate rice to the populace. An unrefined "cottage statistics" of the camp was endeavored, yet an assault on Mak Mun Camp in late March constrained a few thousand outcasts to escape to Nong Samet, refuting the registration.

After two days, powers commanded by the Mak Mun warlord, Van Saren, assaulted Nong Samet in reprisal. In a counterattack on March 22, Van Saren was executed, potentially by the Thai military, and Mak Mun was shut on April 11 by the Thai government trying to merge the populace, the vast majority of which had just migrated to Nong Chan and Nong Samet.

In late May 1980 Nong Samet was moved to a site neighboring the Prasaht Sdok Kok Thom, in a zone with poor waste and landmines left over from a past conflict.

10.3 Incorporation into the KPNLF

On July 12, 1980, troops commanded by Ung Chan Don, In-Sakhan's previous partner, assaulted Nong Samet and drove In-Sakhan to Aranyaprathet, where "on a quiet Sunday evening, In-Sakhan gave up to the Thai Third Infantry Battalion." In-Sakhan was supplanted by Om Luot (otherwise called Ta Luot or Siem Sam On) with Thou Thon going about as non military personnel administrator. Om Luot had proclaimed his dependability to the KPNLF in February 1979, however pressures with General Dien Del and General Sak Sutsakhan in the end prompted Om Luot's homicide on October 11, 1982. After this, Thou Thon became boss administrator of the camp. Nong Samet Camp before long turned into an essential selecting area for Khmer People's National Liberation Armed Forces troops.

10.4 Thou Thon's leadership

Thou Thon was a model of solid yet circumspect regular citizen authority when warlords controlled the majority of the outskirt displaced person populace. As indicated by Linda Mason and Roger Brown, who knew him in 1980:

The Khmer displaced people in Nong Samet Camp owed a lot to him. He had composed the camp—building streets, burrowing trench, tidying up. He had wiped out a significant part of the robbery that had kept the exiles anxious and scared. He had composed a productive conveyance framework with the goal that everybody got rice… He was a diligent employee… When he had sorted out the building of the sustaining focus, he didn't simply guide individuals, he moved up on the roof and began nailing down the cross section chip away at which the cover would be set. At the point when trench were burrowed, he was there with a hoe.

Thou Thon's sibling Colonel Thou Thip had helped to establish the KPNLF in Paris in 1978, together with Son Sann and Dien Del among others. Thou Thon likewise had a sibling and a sister in New Zealand yet he would not acknowledge their sponsorship offers. Not at all like Thou Thip, Thou Thon kept up, best case scenario just a lukewarm association with Son Sann.

In 1983, when Nong Samet was being threatened daily by savage demonstrations of banditry, neighborhood policing was ineffectual to the point that the bandits could gloat about their adventures in the commercial center. At last, after an especially unmitigated demonstration of brutality, three bandits who had recognized themselves in the market the day preceding were found with their throats cut at the edge of the camp. Banditry diminished essentially in camp after this. Thou Thon in this manner exhibited his ability to utilize rundown execution as a methods for looking after request. This made an impression on the camp populace as much as it did to would-be bandits, that security was a need and that it would be enforced.

Thou Thon kept on managing Nong Samet after the camp was joined into Site Two out of 1985.

10.5 Camp migration in 1983

The whole camp was moved again in January 1983 to fairly higher ground only east of the town of Ban Nong Samet, on land viewed as on the Cambodian side of the fringe. This move was encouraged by allegations that Thailand was harboring hostile to socialist guerrillas on its territory, in this manner exasperating the effectively mind boggling political situation.

10.6 Camp population

Nong Samet's official populace gauge in 1979 was more than 100,000, a figure that William Shawcross offers belief to, yet Mason and Brown ascertain that it most likely varied somewhere in the range of 48,00 and 60,000. The American Refugee Committee's 1983 Annual Report numbered the populace at "somewhere in the range of 45,000 and 70,000," in view of nourishment dispersion insights, inoculation records, and birth and demise tallies, anyway this did exclude KPNLF troops, who were absolved from help, and may have comprised an extra 8,000 men.

10.7 Vietnamese evacuees at NW82

As of December 18, 1981, Nong Samet got home to around 700 Vietnamese evacuees who were moved from a unique camp for "land outcasts" who had crossed Cambodia from Vietnam and entered Thailand. They had been moved from the close by camp of NW9 and were housed in a different area known as NW82 or 'the stage' in light of a wooden stage worked to keep the populace off the swampy ground. By September 1982 there were in excess of 1,800 exiles in the swarmed and unsanitary camp. At first Thailand kept remote government offices from talking these displaced people, anyway after rehashed demands by the ICRC, this approach was turned around. The Intergovernmental Committee for Migration led fundamental screening of the 1,804 NW82 Vietnamese and facilitated endeavors of the 15 nations ready to offer resettlement to the evacuees. By January 28, 1983, when the first round of handling was finished, 1,713 of the exiles had gotten resettlement offers. The United States acknowledged a little more than 60 percent.

On February 9, 1983, NW82 was shut, and the staying 122 occupants without resettlement offers were moved briefly to the Khao-I-Dang Holding Center.

10.8 Camp services

Nourishment appropriation issues had been settled by the guide offices in 1980 and Nong Samet turned into a model camp for its association and the nature of its medicinal services administrations, which incorporated a tuberculosis treatment program, set up regardless of cases that the circumstance was still too precarious to allow long haul treatment. A 100-bed emergency clinic with pediatrics, maternity and careful offices and two outpatient centers were worked by the American Refugee Committee, which prepared 150 Khmer doctors, birthing specialists, drug specialists and attendants. Circular segment likewise worked a conventional medication clinic.

Nourishment and some water were given by the World Food Program under the supervision of the United Nations Border Relief Operation (UNBRO). Profound wells additionally gave consumable water to a significant part of the camp.

sanitation and maternal-youngster wellbeing by World Concern, physical restoration by Handicap International, and security by UNBRO. CRS additionally worked a versatile dental group and the Japan International Volunteer Center (JVC) gave a week after week X-beam service.

10.9 Personal memories from help workers

A few guide laborers have portrayed their encounters at Nong Samet Camp, including Dr. Louis Braile:

There was actually a tangible distinction between Nong Samet and KID (Khao-I-Dang Holding Center). Maybe it emerged from the wild climate. Maybe it was the nearness of the old remnants, or maybe it was the way that these individuals, in contrast to the KID occupants, had little any expectation of expatriating.

Dr. Steven H. Miles, Medical Director for the American Refugee Committee, composed:

Help toward the finish of the Khmer Rouge has been supplanted by dread of the present. There is a hard misery here, substantially more so than previously. Break is beyond the realm of imagination. Viciousness and corruption are unavoidable. War is sure. Dread, a feeling of extraordinary powerlessness, is the inescapable feeling.

Robert C. Watchman Jr. of the US Embassy in Bangkok composed:

The Khmer camp at Nong Samet...always held the most outlandish interest and fervor for me.... A tall woodland gave welcome shade. The stone vestiges of an old Angkor-style Buddhist sanctuary gave it an especially Khmer air. While its initial military authority was among the more corrupt, disruptive and vile, the camp was curiously efficient and firmly run.... It had a fascinating populace and an energetic market. For a period in 1979 and 1980 it was the most crowded Cambodian city on earth, far outperforming the then stiring yet at the same time minor Phnom Penh.

Chapter 11: The Vietnamese dry-season offensive of 1984

In April 1984 the Vietnamese started setting up the K-5 outskirt barrier and propelled an assault on Ampil Camp to the upper east of Nong Samet, anyway the KPNLAF held firm, acquiring fortifications and incurring overwhelming losses. The Vietnamese even left 200 of their own men to seep to death on the inclines around the camp. Ampil Camp was pulverized in the battling, driving the KPNLF to migrate its home office. The Vietnamese attacked Nong Chan Camp on November 21 and had occupied the greater part of the abandoned, wore out camp by November 23. Sporadic battling proceeded until the 30th when the KPNLAF pulled back the vast majority of its soldiers to Prey Chan (Site 6).

Nong Samet Camp was assaulted and obliterated by the Vietnamese on Christmas Day, 1984. The assault started with shelling at 5:25 a.m., as per Soth Sour, the watchman at the TB Clinic close to segment 2. KPNLAF troops held bits of the camp for about seven days after this, yet at last it was abandoned. News reports at first asserted that around 100 regular folks had been executed, yet this was later changed to 55 opposition warriors and 63 civilians.

Kenneth Conboy induces that the Vietnamese were on edge to compensate for their humiliating destruction at Ampil in mid 1984, and that this drove them to submit the whole ninth Division in addition to part of another: more than 4,000 men, 18 cannons pieces and 27 T-54 tanks and heavily clad faculty transporters took an interest in this assault.

Various KPNLF troopers and officers, including General Dien Del, announced that during battling at Nong Samet on December 27 the Vietnamese utilized a green-colored "nonlethal however ground-breaking combat zone gas" which staggered its victims and caused queasiness and foaming at the mouth.

11.1Camp movement to Site Two

Upon the arrival of the assault, Nong Samet's populace of 60,000 fled to the Red Hill clearing site and was moved by transport on January 20–22, 1985 to Site 7 (Bang Poo or Bang Phu, "Town of the Crab"), another camp made alongside Khao-I-Dang Holding Center. On September 29 the populace was shipped to Site Two Refugee Camp close to Ta Phraya.

In Site Two, Nong Samet's populace kept up a different area and its own personality, with numerous administrations and quite a bit of its organization unchanged.

Chapter 12 :Nam tiến

Nam tiến alludes to the southward development of the territory of Vietnam from the eleventh century to the mid-eighteenth century. The territory of Vietnam was bit by bit expanded to the south from its unique heartland in the Red River Delta. In a range of somewhere in the range of 700 years, Vietnam significantly increased its territory in size and pretty much gained its stretched state of today.

The bearing of development to the south could be clarified by geographic and statistic factors. With the South China Sea to the east, the Truong Son Mountains to the west, and China to the north, the Vietnamese nation pushed south, after the beach front fields. The 11–fourteenth hundreds of years saw fight increases and misfortunes as the wilderness territory changed hands between the Vietnamese and Chams. In the 15–seventeenth hundreds of years following the bombed Ming victory (1407–1420), the resurgent Vietnamese took the upper hand, vanquishing the less-brought together province of Champa, driving the cession of more land. By the 17–nineteenth hundreds of years, Vietnamese pioneers had infiltrated the Mekong Delta. The Nguyen Lords of Hue by diplomacy and power wrested the southernmost territory from Cambodia, finishing the "Walk to the South".

12.1 History

The local occupants of the Central Highlands are the Degar

(Montagnard People) people groups. Vietnam vanquished and attached the zone during its "walk to the south" (Nam tiến).

Cham areas were seized by the Nguyen Lords. Provinces and locale initially constrained by Cambodia were taken by Vo Vuong.

Cambodia was always attacked by the Vietnamese Nguyen Lords. Around a thousand Vietnamese pioneers were butchered in 1667 in Cambodia by a consolidated power of Chinese and Cambodians. Vietnamese pilgrims began to occupy Mekong Delta that was recently occupied by the Khmer and accordingly the Vietnamese were exposed to Cambodian retaliation. The Cambodians told Catholic European emissaries that the Vietnamese abuse against Catholics supported retaliatory assaults propelled against the Vietnamese colonists.

Vietnamese Emperor Minh Mang instituted the last victory of the Champa Kingdom after the hundreds of years long Cham–Vietnamese wars. The Cham Muslim pioneer Katip Suma was taught in Kelantan and returned to Champa to announce a Jihad against the Vietnamese after Emperor Minh Mang's extension of Champa. The Vietnamese coercively bolstered reptile and pig meat to Cham Muslims and cow meat to Cham Hindus without wanting to rebuff them and acclimatize them to Vietnamese culture.

Minh Mang sinicized ethnic minorities, for example, Cambodians, asserted the inheritance of Confucianism and China's Han tradition for Vietnam, and utilized the term Han individuals 漢人 (Hán nhân) to allude to the Vietnamese. Minh Mang proclaimed that "We should trust that their savage propensities will be subliminally dispersed, and that they will every day become progressively contaminated by Han Sino-Vietnamese customs." These approaches were aimed at the Khmer and slope tribes. The Nguyen master Nguyen Phuc Chu had alluded to Vietnamese as "Han individuals" in 1712 when separating among Vietnamese and Chams. The Nguyen Lords set up đồn điền after 1790. It was said "Hán di hữu hạn" Hán tự: 漢夷有限 ("the Vietnamese and the brutes must have clear outskirts") by the Gia Long Emperor (Nguyễn Phúc Ánh) while separating among Khmer and Vietnamese. Minh Mang executed a cultural assimilation mix strategy coordinated at minority non-Vietnamese peoples. Thanh nhân 清人 or Đường nhân 唐人 were utilized to allude to ethnic Chinese by the Vietnamese while

Vietnamese called themselves as Hán dân Hán tự: 漢民 and Hán nhân Hán tự: 漢人 in Vietnam during the 1800s under Nguyễn rule.

Extraordinary enemy of Vietnamese sentiment because of Vietnam's success of already Cambodian lands which are presently the Mekong delta part of cutting edge Vietnam and many long stretches of Vietnamese intrusions, Vietnamese pioneers in Cambodia and Vietnam's military enslavement of Cambodia, has prompted outrageous enemy of Vietnamese emotions against ethnic Vietnamese in Cambodia and against Vietnam, and thus has prompted ace China sentiment among the Cambodian government and the Cambodian restriction, remembering for the South China Sea, leaving Americans unaware of this to be bewildered by expert China leanings in Cambodia.

Chapter 13 : Vietnamese outskirt strikes in Thailand

After the 1978 Vietnamese attack of Cambodia and consequent breakdown of Democratic Kampuchea in 1979, the counter Hanoi Khmer Rouge fled to the fringe areas of Thailand, and, with help from China, Pol Pot's soldiers figured out how to regroup and redesign in forested and precipitous zones on the Thai-Cambodian outskirt. During the 1980s and mid 1990s Khmer Rouge powers worked from inside displaced person camps in Thailand, trying to de-balance out the star Hanoi People's Republic of Kampuchea's administration, which Thailand would not perceive. Thailand and Vietnam went head to head over the Thai-Cambodian fringe with visit Vietnamese invasions and shellings into Thai territory all through the 1980s in quest for Cambodian guerrillas who continued assaulting Vietnamese occupation powers.

Thailand's doubt of Vietnamese long haul targets and dread of Vietnamese support for an inward Thai socialist uprising development drove the Thai government to support United States destinations in South Vietnam during the Vietnam War.

In 1973 another regular citizen government in Thailand made an opportunity for some level of compromise with North Vietnam, when it proposed to expel United States military powers from Thai soil and receive a more neutralist position. Hanoi reacted by sending a designation to Bangkok, yet talks separated before any advancement in improving relations could be made. Talks continued in August 1976, after Hanoi had crushed the South Vietnamese and joined the nation under its standard. They brought about a require a trade of diplomats and for an opening of dealings on exchange and financial co-activity, however a military coup in October 1976 introduced another Thai government less thoughtful to the Vietnamese socialists. Contact was continued quickly in May 1977, when Vietnam, Thailand, and Laos held a meeting to examine continuing work on the Mekong Development Project, a significant agreeable exertion that had been ended by the Vietnam War. Starting in December 1978, nonetheless, the contention in Cambodia ruled conciliatory trades, and occasional Vietnamese military offensives that included attacks over the Thai outskirt and various Thai setbacks especially stressed the relationship.

In 1979, after Vietnam's military occupation of Cambodia Bangkok aligned itself with the Khmer Rouge, an enemy of Vietnam and sought Beijing for security help. In the two occurrences, Thailand's actions solidified Hanoi's mentality toward Bangkok. As the ASEAN part generally defenseless against a theoretical Vietnamese assault for having offered safe house to the Khmer Rouge in camps inside its territory, Thailand was preeminent among the ASEAN accomplices contradicting Vietnam's 1978 intrusion of Cambodia.

Chapter 14 : Timeline

1979

- October: A significant offensive by the Vietnamese against Khmer

Rouge refuges in their mountain havens pushed thousands of Khmer Rouge warriors, their families and the regular citizens under their influence to the Thai border.

•   8 November: Thai gunnery shoot hit Nong Chan Refugee Camp, executing around 100 displaced people.

•   12 November: Vietnamese assaults inverse Ban Laem drove 5,000 Khmer Rouge troops and residents into Thailand. About half went to Kamput Holding Center.

1980

•   23 June: because of the sorted out repatriation of thousands of outcasts, 200 Vietnamese soldiers crossed the fringe at 02:00 into the Ban Non Mak Mun territory, including Nong Chan Refugee Camp, setting off a three-day big guns fight that left around 200 dead, including around 22–130 Thai officers, one Thai resident, scores of evacuees and roughly 72–100 People's Army of Vietnam (PAVN) troops. Several outcasts were accounted for slaughtered, numerous by a Thai cannons blast that struck one of the camps. Others were trapped in the crossfire. Several hundred evacuees who opposed the Vietnamese were bound and executed. Vietnamese soldiers incidentally held onto two Thai outskirt towns including Ban Non Mak Mun and shelled others.

•   24 June: Still controlling Nong Chan, Vietnamese powers battled mounted guns and little arms duels with Thai soldiers and assaulted guerrilla strongpoints. The Vietnamese shot down two Thai military aircraft.

•   26 June: Vietnamese soldiers held onto two alleviation officials (Robert Ashe and International Committee of the Red Cross (ICRC) Medical Coordinator Dr. Pierre Perrin) and two American photographers at Nong Chan Refugee Camp.

1981

•   4 January: Vietnamese powers stormed over the outskirt, opened shoot with rocket-moved projectiles and automatic weapons, and struggled with Thai soldiers before being pushed back. Two Thai warriors were killed and one was injured during the early morning, hour and a half fight. Somewhere in the range of 50 and 60 Vietnamese troopers allegedly opened fire on a Thai watch a large portion of a mile inside Thailand. Vietnamese setbacks are unknown. Thai troop fortifications were raced to the fringe on the following day and put on alarm against another cross-outskirt attack by Hanoi's troops.

1982

- **Early March: A spate of occurrences along the outskirt, finishing in the interruption of 300 Vietnamese soldiers and the executing of various Thai Border Patrol Police.**

- **21 October: Vietnamese heavy weapons specialists opened shoot on a Thai surveillance plane close to the outskirt, however didn't hit the flying machine. The plane came back to its base inside Thailand.**

1983

- 16 January: Vietnamese soldiers recovered the village of Yeang Dangkum, east of Nong Chan. Radicals from the non-Communist Khmer People's National Liberation Front (KPNLF) caught the village on 26 December and held it as a major aspect of a progression of activities at year's end.

- 21 January: Vietnamese ordnance assault constrained the KPNLF base in the 0'Bok go to move into Thailand. Non-soldiers return toward the month's end.

- 31 January – 1 February: With substantial mounted guns support, 4,000 covering drove Vietnamese soldiers propelled an attack against Nong Chan, one of the biggest displaced person camps on the outskirt, obliterating it. Ground battling was accounted for outside the camp between Vietnamese soldiers situated in Cambodia and around 2,000 KPNLF guerrillas. simultaneously the Vietnamese kept up a consistent blast of shells, rockets and mortars. At any rate 50 shells landed in Thai territory, killing a 66-year-old rancher and harming a few houses and a Buddhist temple. The evacuee populace of around 24,000 fled with obscure losses while MOULINAKA units were forgotten about, and KPNLF powers pulled back following a 36-hour battle. The Khao-I-Dang ICRC medical clinic got more than 100 non military personnel wounded.

- 31 March: 1,000 Vietnamese soldiers, increased by around 600 PRK "individuals' volunteers," assaulted the Khmer Rouge outcast settlements of Phnom Chat and Chamkar Kor, helped by ordnance, rocket, and Soviet T-54 tank fire. Thai officials revealed that the Vietnamese assaults again had brought about "overflows" with Vietnamese mounted guns and mortar shells falling into adjoining Thai territory. Vietnamese soldiers conflicted with Thai powers for a few days, bringing Bangkok into a guarded crusade. Extreme trade of gunnery and tank discharge murdered 30 regular folks and harmed somewhere in the range of 300 people. Around 22,000 Cambodian regular people fled to Thailand for shelter.

•   Early April: PVNA pulverized the camp of Phnom Chat, regular folks cleared to Red Hill. Sihanouk's Camp David was assaulted and regular folks moved to Green Hill. One Thai fly was shot down.

•   3 April: At least 100 Vietnamese soldiers crossed into Thailand and battled hand-to-hand with a Thai fringe watch, murdering five Thai troopers and injuring eight. An ambush on Ampil Camp, the KPNLF home office, fizzled in light of the fact that KPNLF damage units had exploded a few fuel terminals in the weeks preceding the assault, leaving the division shy of diesel and unfit to assemble its armour.

•   27 December: Vietnam moved soldiers, tanks and reinforced work force bearers into a territory close to the eastern fringe of Thailand and was clearly getting ready to assault Cambodian guerrillas. Around 350 Vietnamese soldiers with a few T-54 tanks and heavily clad faculty transporters landed in Thmar Puok town in western Cambodia, 14 miles southeast of the significant base of the non-Communist Cambodian revolutionaries and 16 miles from the Thai boondocks. Thai military and security officials anticipated that Vietnamese powers should start a dry-season offensive against Cambodian guerrillas next month.

•   December: Vietnamese soldiers conflicted with Thai soldiers more than once on land while Vietnam People's Navy gunboats opened discharge on an armada of ten Thai angling trawlers around 20 miles off the southern Vietnamese coast, holding onto five trawlers and catching 130 fishermen.

1984

•   25 March-early April: Hanoi propelled a 12-day cross-outskirt activity into Thai territory in interest Khmer Rouge rebels, utilizing Soviet-made T-54 tank, 130-mm big guns, and some 400–600 soldiers. Accordingly, Thai ordnance and air control must be called into action, bringing about many setbacks on the two sides and the bringing down of another Thai military plane. Vietnam's cross-fringe strike, alongside Thai military and regular citizen losses, was looked into as truly undermining Thailand's security. Minor conflicts happened in the zone of the Khmer Rouge camp, the Chong

Phra Palai Pass connecting Cambodia and Thailand.

•   15 April: Six hundred Vietnamese soldiers of the fifth Division and the eighth Border Defense Regiment initially shelled, at that point entered Ampil Camp, a guerrilla base on the fringe, murdering 85 and injuring around 60 Cambodian civilians. The day break assault was supported by tanks and gunnery. Around 50 ordnance shells landed on Thai territory close to the base of KPNLF guerrillas. In a communicate monitored in Bangkok, guerrillas faithful to Prince Sihanouk said Vietnam included eight contingents inside striking separation of their fortification at Tatum, a settlement simply inside Cambodia's northern outskirt. Thai soldiers had been put on full cognizant to avert an overflow of the fighting.

•   Late May-early June: the Vietnamese Navy over and over assaulted Thai angling trawlers off the Vietnamese coast, bringing about the passings of three Thai anglers.

•   10 August: Vietnamese infantry, APCs and big guns positioned north of Ampil Camp shelled Nong Chan and Ampil, constraining 10,000 KPNLF troops and non military personnel outcasts to escape into Thailand. Since the 15 April fight for Ampil, the KPNLF had recovered control of the camp.

•   6 November: Vietnamese soldiers assaulted a delicately kept an eye on Thai Border Patrol station close Surin on the outskirt. Two Thai troopers were executed, 25 injured and 5 missing in battling for control of Hill 424 at Traveng, 180 miles upper east of Bangkok. About 100 officers from the PAVN 73rd Regiment pushed about a mile into Thai territory yet were later constrained go into Cambodia by Thai powers. A Thai military source said the Vietnamese crossed the fringe in quest for Khmer Rouge guerrillas.

•   18–26 November: Nong Chan Refugee Camp was assaulted by more than 2,000 warriors of the PAVN ninth Division and fell following seven days of fighting, during which 3 Vietnamese chiefs and 66 Cambodian officers of the KPRAF were killed. 30,000 regular people were moved to departure Site 3 (Ang Sila) at that point to Site 6 (Prey Chan).

•   8 December: Nam Yuen, a little camp in eastern Thailand close to the outskirt with Laos, was shelled and emptied.

•   11 December: Sok Sann was shelled and cleared.

•   25 December: Nong Samet Refugee Camp was assaulted at dawn. The whole Vietnamese ninth Infantry Division (more than 4000 men) in addition to 18 cannons pieces and 27 T-54 tanks and protected staff bearers partook in this assault. The Vietnamese conveyed both 105mm and 130mm howitzers, Soviet-fabricated M-46 field weapons with a scope of up to 27 kilometers. KPNLAF guerrillas asserted that 14 Vietnamese tanks and APCs were annihilated during the fighting. An expected 55 opposition warriors and 63 regular citizens kicked the bucket in the assault and 60,000 regular folks were emptied to Red Hill. Approximately 200 war injured were cleared to Khao-I-Dang. Various KPNLAF warriors and officers, including General Dien Del, revealed that during battling at Nong Samet on 27 December the Vietnamese utilized a green-coloured "nonlethal yet ground-breaking combat zone gas

•   31 December: Vietnamese soldiers trapped two Thai Ranger units in Buriram Province, injuring six and nailing them down with little arms fire for more than 24 hours.

1985

•   January–February: An incredible Vietnamese offensive invades for all intents and purposes every single key base of the Cambodian guerrillas along the wilderness, placing the Thais and Vietnamese in face to face encounter along numerous stretches.

•   5 January: Paet Um assaulted and cleared.

•   7–8 January: Five to 6,000 Vietnamese soldiers, supported by big guns and 15 T-54 tanks and 5 APCs, assaulted Ampil (Ban Sangae). Vietnamese soldiers were supported by 400–500 Cambodian KPRAF troops. The assault was gone before by overwhelming big guns barrage, with somewhere in the range of 7,000 and 20,000 shells falling over a 24-hour time span. Nong Chan and Nong Samet were likewise shelled. Ampil camp tumbled to the Vietnamese following a couple of long stretches of battling disregarding General Dien Del's predictions. KPNLAF troops debilitated 6 or 7 tanks however allegedly lost 103 men in combat. San Ro non military personnel populace emptied to Site 1. A Thai A-37 Dragonfly ground assault plane, was shot down over Buriram Province during the fighting, slaughtering one of the two group individuals. During the ambush on Ampil, Thai soldiers safeguarding Hill 37 close to Ban Sangae supported 11 murdered and 19 injured.

•   23–27 January: Dong Ruk and San Ro camps shelled, 18 regular people were killed. Population of 23,000 fled to Site A.

•   28–30 January: Vietnamese cannons discharged around one hundred

130mm shells, mortars and rockets at places of the Khmer Rouge's 320th Division close to the Khao Din Refugee Camp around 34 miles south of Aranyaprathet. This was trailed by an infantry ambush on Khao Ta-ngoc.

•	13 February: Nong Pru, O'Shallac and Taprik (South of Aranyaprathet) assaulted and emptied to Site 8.

•	16 February: In an engagement with non-socialist revolutionary powers close to Ta Phraya, four Vietnamese rockets containing toxic gas were terminated, making Thai residents in the territory grumble of tipsiness and regurgitating. A Thai Army laboratory affirmed that the rockets contained phosgene gas.

•	18 February: 300 Vietnamese soldiers attacked Khmer Rouge positions close Khlong Nam Sai, 19 miles southeast of Aranyaprathet. Battling started with little arms trades and swelled into a Vietnamese blast with overwhelming cannons and mortars. Thai soldiers discharged warning shots at Vietnamese troopers as they crossed the outskirt in quest for escaping Khmer Rouge guerrillas. One Thai resident was killed.

•	20 February: Vietnamese and Thai warriors battled on Hill 347, about a large portion of a mile inside Thailand's northeastern region of Buriram. A Thai officer was slaughtered and two troopers were injured in the battling, which incorporated a mounted guns duel over the border.

•	5 March: Tatum assaulted. Green Hill populace cleared to Site B. Dong Ruk, San Ro, Ban Sangae, and Vietnamese Land Refugees are altogether moved to Site 2. Somewhere in the range of 1,000 Vietnamese soldiers were consistently encroaching into Thai territory in endeavors to outmaneuver units of the Cambodian obstruction groups.

•	6 March: Thai soldiers and air ship constrained Vietnamese soldiers to withdraw from one of three slopes on Thai territory which the Vietnamese had caught during going before days.

•	7 March: Thai armed force troops supported by cannons and A-37 Dragonfly air ship recovered three slopes seized by encroaching Vietnamese fighters. Several Vietnamese were said to have been driven back over the outskirt into Cambodia. Be that as it may, the Vietnamese counterattacked against Hill 361 on Thai soil behind the attacked Cambodian guerrilla base at Tatum, and the consequences of the fight were not promptly clear. 14 Thai officers and 15 Thai regular folks had been killed.

- 4 April: A conflict happened at Laem Nong Ian, after five Vietnamese interrupted around 875 yards into Thailand.

- 6 April: Thai Border cops killed a Vietnamese officer in Thailand during a 10-minute battle close the border.

- 20 April: At southeastern Thailand's Trat Province, somewhere in the range of 1,200 Vietnamese soldiers assaulted Thai positions arranged 3 to 4 km from the Gulf of Thailand. Rather than pulling back the Vietnamese set up a perpetual base on a slope in Thailand, about a half-mile from the fringe, where they laid mines and fabricated dugouts. Afterward, raising Thai assaults had driven a portion of the Vietnamese go into Cambodia, yet the Vietnamese dispatched a new unit of 600 to 800 men to fortify the hilltop.

- 10 May: A Thai trooper was murdered in the wake of stepping on a land mine while on patrol.

- 11 May: Thai stream warriors and overwhelming ordnance beat Vietnamese soldiers occupying a slope a large portion of a mile inside Thailand, and Thai officers balanced for an ambush on the vigorously mined position. The Thais besieged and shelled the Vietnamese before an infantry activity was to be propelled in the Banthad Mountain run, 170 miles southeast of Bangkok. The Vietnamese were dove in along the slope and had laid a series of mines to counter any Thai ground ambushes. Seven Thai troopers were slaughtered and in any event 16 harmed. Radio Hanoi revealed a Vietnamese Foreign Ministry proclamation denying the most recent announced invasion into Thailand. Thailand blamed Vietnam for in any event 40 cross-fringe raids looking for Cambodian guerrillas since November 1984, however the Vietnamese government had denied the charges.

- 15 May: Vietnamese and Thai troopers conflicted for around eight hours with mortars, antitank guns and automatic rifles.

- 17 May: Thai officers drove barging in Vietnamese warriors again into Cambodia in extreme battling along Thailand's southeastern outskirt. After over seven days of battling, Thai officers and marines held onto part of a Vietnamese-occupied slope simply inside the Thai outskirt the past days.

- May: A rough 230,000 Khmer regular folks were in impermanent clearings in Thailand after an exceptionally effective Vietnamese dry season offensive.

- 26 May: Vietnamese warriors crossed into the Thai region of Ubon Ratchathani from northern Cambodia, clearly scanning for Cambodian guerrillas. A Vietnamese power killed five Thai warriors and a non military personnel in a one-hour conflict with Thai outskirt watches in upper east Thailand. The battling incited Thai common specialists to empty around 600 regular citizens from two outskirt towns to more secure territories in the Nam Yuen district.

- 13 June: Thai powers fought 400 Vietnamese soldiers who crossed into Thailand.

1986

- 23 January: A Vietnamese flood was focused on a Thai marine station in Haad Lek, a town at the southern tip of the fringe. The Vietnamese fire originated from a slope sitting above Haad Lek, inside Cambodian territory. "This seems, by all accounts, to be a purposeful incitement by the Vietnamese", a Thai Navy representative said. "It doesn't resemble an overflow of battling inside Cambodia." A Thai warship in the Gulf of Thailand reacted by shelling the Vietnamese big guns base. The warship discharged in excess of 100 shells and the Vietnamese more than 70 shells.

- 25 January: Vietnamese substantial weapons beat a Thai fringe post, slaughtering three Marines and causing a big guns fight with a Thai warship offshore.

- 7 December: Vietnamese soldiers warned Thailand against proceeding to support Cambodian guerrillas. An amplifier communicate and pamphlets shot from gun close Aranyaprathet District engaged Thailand to decline haven to the guerrillas and warned that it would bear the "results" in the event that it refuses.

1987

- 25 March: Thai Army Commander-in-Chief General Chavalit Yongchaiyudh reports a full scale offensive against Vietnamese soldiers who have barged in into Thai territory past the set 5 km limit.

- 17 April: Thai powers attempted to expel Vietnamese infantry from Chong Bok, an uneven district where the fringes of Thailand, Laos and Cambodia combine. Setbacks in twofold figures are accounted for on both sides.

- 30 May: Thai Rangers watch the Chong Bok locale where battling has seethed to oust Vietnamese from settled in positions simply inside Thai territory.

- Mid-1987: The 800-kilometer Thai-Cambodian outskirt was completely garrisoned by Vietnamese and Cambodian forces.

1988

- 22 April: Vietnamese soldiers crossed the fringe and trapped an organization of outskirt police, slaughtering four Thai officers and injuring another. The organization of five Thai police was watching a key point close to the outskirt in Buriram Province, 174 miles east of Bangkok, when a Vietnamese trooper heaved an explosive into the group and opened shoot with rifles. The Vietnamese warriors were in excess of 500 yards inside Thai territory when they organized the attack.

- 12 June: At around 9 a.m., Vietnamese 105mm and 85mm cannons shelled a Thai town, murdering two locals and injuring two others. Six mounted guns shells struck four miles somewhere inside Thailand.

- 4 August: The pioneer of the Chart Thai Party, General Chatichai Choonhavan, turns into the seventeenth Prime Minister of Thailand, he guarantees "to transform front lines into commercial centers".

1989edit

- 26 April: Vietnamese soldiers discharged four gunnery shells into Site Two, the biggest of the Cambodian evacuee camps with a populace of more than 198,000. Three individuals were seriously injured. After the shelling, the camp was purportedly shut to Western guide officials, including individuals from the United Nations Border Relief Operation, which gave help to the camp.

- September–December: Vietnamese soldiers pulled back from Cambodia.

Chapter 15 : Aftermath

On 14 January 1985, Hun Sen was named Prime Minister of the People's Republic of Kampuchea and started harmony chats with the factions of the Coalition Government of Democratic Kampuchea. Between 2–4 December

1987, Hun Sen met with Sihanouk at Fère-en-Tardenois in France to talk about the eventual fate of Kampuchea. Further talks happened between 20–21 January 1988, and Hun Sen offered Sihanouk a situation inside the Kampuchean Government relying on the prerequisite that he came back to Kampuchea straight away. However, Sihanouk didn't acknowledge the offer, even as arrangements were made in Phnom Penh to get him. Notwithstanding that disappointment, Hun Sen's Kampuchean Government had the option to convince Cheng Heng and In Tam, the two priests in Lon Nol's system, to come back to Kampuchea. In the primary significant advance towards restoring harmony in Kampuchea, agents of the CGDK and the PRK met just because at the First Jakarta Informal Meeting on 25 July 1988. In that gathering, Sihanouk proposed a three-arrange plan, which required a truce, an UN peacekeeping power to supervise the withdrawal of Vietnamese soldiers and the coordination of all Kampuchean outfitted factions into a solitary army.

In this manner, to start the way toward restoring harmony, the Vietnamese designation proposed a two-arrange plan that started with inner exchanges among the Kampuchean factions, trailed by a roundtable dialog with every included nation. The Vietnamese proposition won out at the gathering, yet no understandings were reached. At the Second Jakarta Meeting, on 19 February 1989, Australian Foreign Minister Gareth Evans forwarded the Cambodian Peace Plan to achieve a truce, a peacekeeping power and the foundation of a national solidarity government to keep up Kampuchea's sway until races were held. To encourage a harmony concession to the eve of the Vietnamese withdrawal, between 29–30 April 1989, Hun Sen met a gathering of the National Assembly to receive another constitution, and the nation was renamed the State of Cambodia to mirror the condition of uncertainty of the nation's sovereignty. Furthermore, Buddhism was restored as the state religion, and residents were ensured the privilege to hold private property.

Meanwhile, be that as it may, harmony talks between the warring factions proceeded, with the First Paris Peace Conference on Cambodia held in Paris in 1989. On 26 February 1990, after the withdrawal of Vietnamese soldiers, the Third Jakarta Informal Meeting was held, at which the Supreme National Council was built up to shield Cambodian sway. At first, the Supreme National Council was to have 12 individuals, with three seats designated to every faction of the CGDK, and three to the ace Vietnam Kampuchean People's Revolutionary Party. However, Hun Sen protested the proposed game plan, calling rather for every faction of the CGDK to be given two seats for a total of six, and the Kampuchean People's Revolutionary Party to have six seats. In 1991 the Supreme National Council started speaking to Cambodia at the UN General Assembly. At that point, in an intense move, Hun Sen renamed the Kampuchean People's Revolutionary Party as the Cambodian People's Party with an end goal to depict his gathering as a democratic establishment and revoke its progressive struggle.

On 23 October 1991, the Cambodian factions of the Supreme National Council, alongside Vietnam and 15 part countries of the International Peace Conference on Cambodia, consented to the Paris Peace Arrangement. For the Cambodian individuals, two many years of ceaseless warfare and 13 years of common war appeared to be finished, albeit an air of uneasiness among the pioneers of the Cambodian factions remained. In request to incorporate the Khmer Rouge in the understanding, the significant forces consented to abstain from utilizing "decimation" to depict the actions of the Government of Democratic Kampuchea in the period somewhere in the range of 1975 and 1979. Subsequently, Hun Sen condemned the Paris Agreement as being a long way from great, as it neglected to help the Cambodian individuals to remember the abominations submitted by the Khmer Rouge regime. Nonetheless, the Paris Agreement set up the United Nations Transitional Authority in Cambodia (UNTAC), as per the UN Security Council's Resolution 745, and gave UNTAC an expansive mandate to supervise primary strategies and organization works until a Cambodian government was democratically elected.

On 14 November 1991, Sihanouk came back to Cambodia to take an interest in the decisions, trailed by Son Senn, a Khmer Rouge official, who showed up a couple of days after the fact to set up the association's electoral battle office in Phnom Penh. On 27 November 1991, Khieu Samphan likewise came back to Cambodia on a departure from Bangkok; at first he had anticipated that his appearance should be uneventful, yet when Khieu Samphan's flight landed at Pochentong Airport, he was met by an irate group which yelled put-down and maltreatment at him. As Khieu Samphan was crashed into the city, another group lined the course towards his office and tossed objects at his car. As soon as he landed at his office, Khieu Samphan entered and promptly called the Chinese Government to spare him. In no time afterwards, an irate horde constrained its way into the building, pursued Khieu Samphan up the subsequent floor and attempted to balance him from a roof fan. In the long run, Khieu Samphan had the option to escape from the building by a stepping stool with his face bloodied, and was quickly taken to Pochentong Airport, where he flew out of Cambodia. With the takeoff of Khieu Samphan, the Khmer Rouge's investment in the political decision appeared doubtful.

In March 1992, the beginning of the UNTAC crucial Cambodia was set apart by the appearance of 22,000 UN peacekeepers, which included soldiers from 22 nations, 6,000 officials, 3,500 police and 1,700 non military personnel workers and electoral volunteers. The strategic drove by Yasushi Akashi. In June 1992, the Khmer Rouge officially settled the National Union Party of Kampuchea, and declared that it would not enroll to take an interest in the upcoming races. Moreover, the Khmer Rouge likewise would not incapacitate its powers as per the Paris agreement. Then, to keep ethnic Vietnamese from participating in the races, the Khmer Rouge began slaughtering Vietnamese non military personnel networks, making a huge number of Vietnamese escape Cambodia. Towards the finish of 1992, Khmer Rouge powers progressed into Kampong Thom so as to increase a key a dependable balance, before UN peacekeeping powers were completely conveyed there. In the months paving the way to the races, a few UN military watches were assaulted as they entered Khmer Rouge-held territory.

In spite of progressing dangers from the Khmer Rouge during the decisions, on 28 May 1993, FUNCINPEC won 45.47 percent of the vote, against 38.23 percent for the Cambodian People's Party. Though plainly vanquished, Hun Sen would not acknowledge the consequences of the political race, so his Defense Minister, Sin Song, declared the severance of the eastern territories of Cambodia, which hosted supported the Cambodian People's Gathering. Ruler Norodom Ranariddh, pioneer of FUNCINPEC and child of Sihanouk, consented to frame an alliance government with the Cambodian People's Party so the nation would not separate. On 21 September 1993, the Cambodian Constituent Assembly endorsed another Constitution and Ranariddh turned out to be First Prime Minister. He designated Hun Sen as the Second Prime Minister. On 23 September 1993, the protected government was restored with Norodom Sihanouk as the head of state. In July 1994, the Cambodian Government prohibited the Khmer Rouge for its persistent infringement of the Paris Agreement. Most fundamentally, the Cambodian Government additionally explicitly perceived the slaughter and outrages which happened under Democratic Kampuchea. By 1998, the Khmer Rouge was totally dissolved.

Vietnam rejoins the world

The military occupation of Kampuchea had profound ramifications for Vietnamese international strategy. Since picking up autonomy in 1954, the Vietnamese socialist viewpoint on international strategy had been ruled by the need to keep up a world request of two camps, socialist and non-communist. Indeed, the arrangements of kinship that Vietnam marked with the Soviet Union, Laos and the People's Republic of Kampuchea were reliable with that view. Notwithstanding, the ideological inspirations of the Vietnamese socialist authority were demonstrated to be constrained and vigorously imperfect, as showed by the 1979 judgment of Vietnam in the wake of expelling the Khmer Rouge regime. In the years that pursued, the Vietnamese Government was left segregated from the world and its endeavors to rebuild the nation were handicapped by the absence of help from the entrepreneur Western countries. Besides, the nearness of Vietnamese military powers in Cambodia turned into a hindrance which anticipated the standardization of strategic ties with China, the United States and the part countries of ASEAN.

Considering the decay experienced by the Soviet Union and the communist nations of Eastern Europe, the Vietnamese Government started fixing discretionary relations with neighboring nations as a major aspect of a more prominent exertion to restore Vietnam's broken economy. Since its attack in 1979, China had put supported weight on the northern fringes of Vietnam, with the region of Ha Tuyen consistently shelled by Chinese big guns. In September 1985, Chinese assault of Ha Tuyen arrived at a pinnacle when 2,000 rounds were fired. To decrease the condition of threatening vibe along the fringe locale, and at last standardize relations with China, the Vietnamese Government dropped every unfriendly reference to China at the sixth

National Party Congress in December 1986, and additionally embraced the Doi Moi policy. In August 1990, as the Cambodian Peace Plan, created by Australian Foreign Minister Gareth Evans, was being supported by the UN Security Council, both China and Vietnam moved towards accommodation.

Right off the bat in September 1990, Vietnamese Prime Minister Đỗ Mười, general secretary Nguyen Van Linh and previous Prime Minister Pham Van Dong headed out to Chengdu, China, where they held a mystery meeting with Chinese Prime Minister Li Peng and General Secretary of the Chinese Communist Party Jiang Zemin. On 17 September 1990, General Võ Nguyên Giáp likewise made an outing to China and expressed gratitude toward the Chinese Government for its past assistance. Despite outward indications of progress in Vietnam's discretionary relations with China, Vietnamese pioneers were hesitant to embrace any harmony plan which could debilitate their customer system in Phnom Penh. Be that as it may, as the four Cambodian factions agreed on the power-sharing course of action laid out at the Third Jakarta Informal Meeting in February 1990, Vietnam and China quickly moved to restore formal political relations. In November 1991, recently chose Vietnamese Prime Minister Võ Văn Kiệt went to Beijing and met his Chinese partner, Li Peng, and they gave a 11-point report restoring conciliatory ties between the two nations following 10 years without formal relations.

The finish of the Cambodian clash likewise finished the ASEAN-forced exchange and help ban which had been set up since 1979. In January 1990, Thai Prime Minister Chatichai Choonhavan openly voiced his support for Vietnam, and the remainder of Indochina, to pick up induction into ASEAN. In the period between late 1991 and mid 1992, Vietnam restored relations with a few part countries of ASEAN. Subsequently, somewhere in the range of 1991 and 1994, ventures from ASEAN nations made up 15 percent of direct outside interest in Vietnam. Aside from the undeniable financial advantages, ASEAN additionally gave a tranquil situation that ensured Vietnam's national protection from remote dangers in the post-Cold War time, when Soviet guide was no longer available. Thus, on 28 July 1995, Vietnam officially turned into the seventh individual from ASEAN, in the wake of driving ASEAN officials welcomed Vietnam to join at the ASEAN

Ministerial Meeting in Bangkok in 1994. Then, in August 1995, the U.S. Contact Office in Hanoi was upgraded to Embassy status, after U.S. President Bill Clinton declared a conventional standardization of conciliatory relations with Vietnam on 11 July 1995, in this manner finishing Vietnam's disconnection from the United States.

Natural impacts

Cambodia and Vietnam's timberland spread experienced extreme decreases following the finish of the Khmer Rouge regime. The fall of Khmer Rouge was credited to Vietnamese soldiers toppling the legislature and the occupation of Phnom Penh, setting up the People's Republic of Kampuchea (PRK) in 1978. With absence of universal support before the finish of the Cold War, the Khmer Rouge attempted to rebuild itself. In an endeavor to expand income and recover control, they built up themselves along the Thailand-Cambodia outskirt in northwestern Cambodia to concentrate on misusing Cambodia's normal assets incorporating timber and rubies. With 15% of total worldwide tropical backwoods, Southeast Asia is a pioneer in timber production. This activity immediately turned into a race between political factions, as the PRK embraced Khmer Rouge extraction efforts.

From 1969 to 1995, Cambodia's backwoods spread shrank from 73% to 30–35%. Similarly, Vietnam lost almost 3,000,000 hectares of woods spread from 1976 to 1995. In 1992, Khmer Rouge turned out to be universally isolated. The United Nations Security Council prohibited all fares of Cambodian timber in November of that year. Efforts to make an impartial electoral condition prompted the foundation of the United Nations Transitional Authority (UNTAC) in Cambodia. The move was executed in January 1993. around the same time, the Vietnamese gave a logging boycott, driving the Khmer Rouge to logging illegally. Illicit fares from Cambodia to Vietnam was worth US$130 million each year.

Thailand was the biggest violator of UNTAC. The Thai government at the time demanded that Cambodian imported timber must have an authentication of beginning endorsed by the administrative experts in Phnom Penh. These declarations cost US$35 for each cubic meter of timber from Khmer Rouge working areas. This constrained the Khmer Rouge to expand costs. They figured out how to communicate in Thai and sold timber wrongfully to Thai timber operators, acquiring them over US$10 million monthly. Global Witness, a worldwide human rights and natural non-legislative association (NGO) situated in London, perceived these timber guerillas when they distinguished mass Cambodian exports. They in this way campaigned for a correction to the US Foreign Operations Act. The demonstration was passed. It expressed that US help would never again be given to any nation collaborating militarily with the Khmer Rouge. Thailand shut its fringes with Cambodia the following day.

Japan was the second biggest offender of UNTAC, buying 8,000 cubic meters of timber from Cambodia. There were 46 other distinguished offenders including the Koreas, Singapore, and Taiwan. After timber is created by Cambodia or the more prominent Southeast Asia locale, these "offender" nations re-process the logs which are in this manner moved to North America, the Middle East, and Africa for sale.

PRK inevitably offered the Khmer Rouge re-joining into Cambodia's national military just as compromise between the two parties. In August 1996, the territorial command of Khmer Rouge went back to Phnom Penh. Pol Pot, the previous Prime Minister of the Democratic Kampuchea, and his lieutenants remained in the northern locale to proceed with endeavors at producing income from the extraction of characteristic resources. However, the group got superfluous because of an absence of support. By 1998, Khmer Rouge had disintegrated completely.

In 2010, the Royal Government of Cambodia set out a timberland the executives plan called the National Forest Program (NFP) so as to deal with Cambodia's backwoods industry successfully in the long-term. various contributors had been in support of the United Nations Program on Reducing emanations from deforestation and woodland debasement (UN-REDD). UN-REDD itself contributed over US$3 million. The task has likewise been financed by the United Nations Development Program through Target for Resource Assignment from the Core (UNDP-TRAC) with US$500,000, the

9 7 9 8 7 4 6 3 0 1 5 6 7